From Ballots to Mugshots
A Study of Political Corruption, Crime, and Consequences in the U.S.

by Thomas T. Taylor

Copyright 2023 Archieboy Holdings, LLC.
All rights reserved.

Formatted, Converted, and Distributed by eBookIt.com
http://www.eBookIt.com

ISBN-13: 9781456641948 (paperback)
ISBN-13: 9781456641931 (ebook)
ISBN-13: 9781456641955 (audiobook)

No part of this book may be reproduced in any form or by any electronic or mechanical means including information storage and retrieval systems, without permission in writing from the author. The only exception is by a reviewer, who may quote short excerpts in a review.

Although the author and publisher have made every effort to ensure that the information in this book was correct at press time, the author and publisher do not assume and hereby disclaim any liability to any party for any loss, damage, or disruption caused by errors or omissions, whether such errors or omissions result from negligence, accident, or any other cause.

This publication is designed to provide accurate and authoritative information with regard to the subject matter covered. It is sold with the understanding that the publisher is not engaged in rendering professional services. If legal advice or other expert assistance is required, the services of a competent professional should be sought.

The fact that an organization or website is referred to in this work as a citation and/or a potential source of further information does not mean that the author or the publisher endorses the information the organization or website may provide or recommendations it may make.

Please remember that Internet websites listed in this work may have changed or disappeared between when this work was written and when it is read.

Dear Esteemed Reader,

Thank you immensely for choosing this book to join your collection. We imagine that you've already embarked on an exploration of ideas within these pages, and we couldn't be happier about it!

Now, if you find yourself chuckling, pondering, or even debating with the words in front of you, we'd absolutely love to hear about it. If you can spare a few moments to pen down your thoughts in a review, we would be as delighted as a dictionary on a spelling bee!

An Amazon review would be excellent - but hey, we're far from picky. Whether it's a scribble on the back of a grocery list, a tweet, or even a message in a bottle (though that might take a while to reach us), your feedback is gold.

Writing a review might not be as fun as a spontaneous dance-off, but we promise it'll bring grins to our faces, warmth to our hearts, and incredibly valuable insights to future readers.

With Gratitude,

Bo Bennett, PhD
Publisher
Archieboy Holdings, LLC.

Table of Contents

Foreword

As you delve into the pages of this book, the aim is to subtly reset your perspectives and attitudes toward the ever-complex world of politics. It's a topic that's often viewed in only black and white. However, this book caters to unveil the breathtaking array of grays that blanket this myriad subject.

I am writing this foreword to assure the reader that the purpose of this book is not to shame any particular individuals, nor will any specific politicians be mentioned directly. Instead, the focus here is on the larger systems and mechanisms at play that, unexamined, can foster corruption or misconduct.

That's not to suggest that this book is a dry, abstract study. Far from it. Over these pages, you will find references to real charges brought against notable politicians by dedicated prosecutors. While individual names are withheld, these cases present a wide variety of real situations and challenges faced by our leaders, our justice system, and ourselves as informed citizens.

While it can be tempting to paint all politicians with a broad, cynical brush, it's essential to remember that most individuals in public office are driven by a real desire to serve their constituents and their nation. That doesn't mean, however, that they're immune to making mistakes or succumbing to less noble temptations.

Our journey will begin by examining the allure of power. Understanding this aspect is crucial because the deceptive shimmer of power is at the heart of virtually all instances of political misconduct. We'll delve into the psychological effects, the road to public office, and the changing shifts in the American politics landscape.

Our subsequent voyage will take us through the various types of crimes that have historically enveloped renowned politicians. From gross misuse of finance to the abuse of power, instances of particular failings, as well as high crimes, will be discussed. While keeping the discourse strictly educational and constructive, you'll acquire an understanding of these offenses in a political context.

We'll also examine in depth the mechanisms of corruption, presenting you with a firsthand view of how lobbyists, campaign finances, and the potentially dubious power of patronage work behind the scenes. To truly comprehend the puzzle of corruption, we need to understand each piece, each player, and each method employed.

As to the judicial process, this subject matter too, will feature extensively in the book. After all, the path to the courtroom is often more circuitous and less clear for public figures. Additionally, we'll explore the consequences of a conviction, including the impact it can have on personal, social, and political lives.

We won't stop at merely discussing corruption and the various mechanisms that fuel it. In the final sections of the book, we shall look at the ways to stem this malaise. The role of ethics committees, media and indeed, we the voters, in holding representatives to the highest standard will be extensively deliberated. We'll end our journey with a holistic view of the lessons we've learned, both about the challenges within our political system and the potential it holds for true reform.

This book is not intended to alarm or dishearten you. On the contrary, it is meant to enlighten and even entertain. It's easy to focus on the scandals and the sensational headlines, but it's crucial to remember that they represent only one part of the broader political landscape. They're the anomalies that prove the rules, rather than the norm.

Not every representative will falter, and not every law will be broken. But when those unfortunate cases occur, understanding the causes and effects can provide us with the tools needed to prevent such situations in the future, and perhaps even turn our disillusionment into action.

So, let us embark on this journey of revelation, understanding and empowerment together. After all, we are the citizens, and this is our democracy. When the curtain of uncertainty is lifted, trust and faith take root, making way for better governance and a more promising future.

Get ready, America. This quintessential fascinating tour into the depths of our politics is just about to take off.

Chapter 1:
The Allure of Power

At its core, the allure of power is a universal calling, which, like a siren's song, seduces individuals from all walks of life. In the realm of American politics, the chase for authority becomes a tantalizing quest, the magnetism of which lies in the very ability to reshape landscapes, redraw borders, and manifest ideological visions into tangible realities. What is often underrated is the itch, that almost carnal desire to influence, to matter, and to make a difference, that sets this journey towards power into motion. Politicians, despite their diverse backgrounds and perspectives, share this common trait—a desire to hold the steering wheel of the American narrative. They stand at the forefront of the public eye, prepared to walk a path that promises unparalleled influence and authority, but also potential disgrace and downfall. The inherent contradiction in these outcomes is an integral part of the allure; it's not just about winning, but also about navigating the complexity and vagueness of political ethics. This initial chapter aims to dissect the captivation that power presents, providing a foundation for understanding the subsequent choices, both moral and immoral, that politicians often face on their road to public office. As we delve into this magnetic pull that positions power as the ultimate political prize, we lay the groundwork for exploring the dark underbelly that frequently accompanies this restless pursuit of authority.

The Landscape of American Politics

The mosaic of American politics is as diverse and complicated as the nation itself. From the federal behemoth in Washington, D.C., to the smallest local boards and commissions, every level of the political landscape is peppered with intriguing dynamics and distinct characteristics. It's this amount of variety and versatility that, at its best, can create a robust, flexible system, responsive to a multitude of needs and desires among the population.

Yet, this complexity also creates opportunities for distortion, corruption, and inequity. Power, if unchecked or unbalanced, can corrode the best of intentions, a caveat particularly important in the political sphere, where authority and influence are the currencies of the realm. Recognizing this, it's crucial to comprehend the structure and complexity of American politics.

At the national level, a tripartite system shares decision-making and legislative power among the executive, legislative, and judicial branches. Executive power rests with the President, who is overseen by a bicameral Congress, comprising the Senate and the House of Representatives, as the legislative branch. The judiciary, led by the nine Supreme Court Justices, interprets the laws and ensures their constitutional soundness. This check-and-balance system was carefully crafted by the founding fathers to hinder just any one body or individual from gaining too much control.

When we descend to the state level, similar structures exist. Each state has its own governor and bicameral legislature (except Nebraska, the lone unicameral), along with its separate court system. These entities deal with laws and regulations that specifically pertain to the residents and businesses of their respective states.

Beyond state governments, county and municipal structures play crucial roles in the daily lives of citizens. Here, the intricacies of American politics become even more diverse. These are the realms of school boards, county supervisors, and city commissions, the often-overlooked, yet fundamentally essential components of the democratic machine. These bodies basically serve as the frontlines of governance impacting education, land use, criminal justice at the local level, and much more.

It's within this complex web of political bodies and roles, from the White House to the local PTA, that power winds, bends, and occasionally, snaps. It's here, where vested interests, agendas, and authority intersect, that the potential for corruption can dwell.

Understanding the nature of this landscape is the first step towards potential reform or strengthening. There's no one-size-fits-all approach in such a diverse environment. What may work for a small township in rural Montana may not be applicable to the bustling metropolis of Los Angeles. This inherent variability is why it's vital to appreciate the nuances of the ever-changing political landscape.

Yet, despite the diversity, certain common threads unite this patchwork of governing bodies. One such factor is the democratic underpinning of most roles, in which representatives are elected by the citizens they serve. This introduces contention and competition into the equation, but also a level of accountability.

Election cycles, designed to maintain a fresh rotation of representatives and ideas, both preserve and challenge the status quo. They bring the promise of change or the guarantee of stability, depending on voters' desires at the moment. Yet, they can also become magnets for power brokerages and manipulative practices.

This continuous ebb and flow of power within the American political landscape is a natural outcome of its democratic nature. But it's the manner in which these shifting dynamics are handled that can make the difference between a healthy, effective system and one mired in dysfunction and corruption.

Throughout history, American politics has been a dialogue between progress and conservatism, change and tradition, the collective and the individual. It's neither a smooth nor straightforward journey. Infighting, partisanship, and even scandal are recurring themes. They are, perhaps, to be expected in a sphere where interests are divergent, stakes are high, and the potential for power is omnipresent.

Ultimately, the landscape of American politics, complex as it may be, is crafted by the people, for the people. Each election cycle, protest, and policy debate are the lifeblood of the political organism, keeping it alive, responsive, and perpetually evolving. It's a living entity, shaped by its constituents, influenced by the challenges of its times, and capable of both inspiring progress and igniting controversy.

The Road to Public Office: A Primer

What drives someone to do more than just vote? The allure of power, the prospect of shaping a society, and the pursuit of personal passions all culminate in the decision to embark on the road towards public office. There's a journey involved; a process that's both complex and laden with numerous challenges and demands. Nonetheless, it's an endeavor filled with immeasurable rewards for those who are dedicated, resilient, well-informed, and principled.

Firstly, it's crucial to understand the levels of public office: local, state, and federal. Each level represents diverse roles, tasks, and responsibilities that contribute to the governance of our society. Local offices include positions like city council members, mayors, township trustees, and county officials. Importance is placed on regional concerns and interests.

State roles, such as state representatives, senators, and governors, hold greater influence and bear greater responsibilities. They shape state laws and execute decisions that affect all residents within their respective states. Federal offices include members of Congress, Senators, and of course, the President of the United States. Holding a federal office involves significant policy-making, regulating interstate matters, and addressing national and international concerns.

Setting sights on a specific level of public office demands an understanding of one's interests, strengths, and passions. It's not just about possessing the desire to lead, but also about knowing where and how to foster genuine impact.

Another essential step on the road to public office is understanding the structure of American politics. The two-party system features Democrats and Republicans as principal political entities. Each party has its own ideologies, policy priorities, and constituencies. Having a clear political outlook, and aligning your views and values with one of the parties, serves as an important stepping stone to public office.

For those who choose to tread this path, acquiring relevant knowledge and honing essential skills form crucial baselines.

This includes nurturing a deep understanding of public policy, law, governance, leadership, negotiation, diplomacy and, of course, the ability to communicate effectively - to articulate visions, inspirations and rational thought to the public.

Running for public office also entails putting oneself out there in a public, and often monumental, way. It's not just about having a noticeable and assertive presence, but also the ability to weather criticism and scrutiny. This involves coalition-building, creating a robust campaign strategy, and being comfortable enough to expose personal and professional backgrounds for public scrutiny.

One common misconception is that holding a public office is a one-man endeavor. It's not. A successful run demands a strong team, committed volunteers, and an extensive network capable of providing financial, emotional, and professional support. A good leader acknowledges the importance of relationships, networking, and team dynamics.

The legal process, though seemingly daunting, is an inherent part of this journey. To qualify as a candidate, there's a requirement to fulfill certain criteria and procedural steps. This might include filing official forms, adhering to campaign finance regulations, and meeting residency, age, or citizenship requirements.

The road to public office is also paved with financial implications. Funding campaigns is part of the deal. Understanding its nuances – from raising funds to managing them effectively and legally – is vital.

Lastly, it's fundamentally about representing constituents. Public office holders must resonate with their community, understanding their concerns and aspirations. This requires conducting extensive demographic research, fostering active community connections, and regular dialogues with constituents.

The navigation of this demanding journey demands the qualities of resilience, conviction, principles, diplomacy, and the art of negotiation. It's not a path for the faint-hearted. Yet, despite its immense challenges, the rewards of public service can be incomparable – the opportunity to make impactful decisions, the authority to change laws, and the potential to shape society's destiny.

The role is not merely about personal achievement, but about serving the public, enhancing societal good, and shaping the direction of a country. The path may be arduous, but the potential rewards – the ability to alter the course of history and the future of millions – are uniquely inspiring and fulfilling.

As with any great endeavor, the road to public office is better travelled with knowledge as your compass and principle as your North Star. The responsibility of shaping the future of the American people starts with understanding that the road to public office is not for the achievement of personal glory but for the dedication to public service.

The Psychology of Power and How It Changes People

Power is perhaps one of the most pervasive facets of our existence; it shapes our relationships, our societies, and indeed, our very understanding of the world around us. But what is the psychology of power, and how does it alter the people who wield it?

No stranger to the dynamics of authority, Sigmund Freud posited that the pursuit of power is a principal motivator of human behavior. Freud believed that the human psyche is essentially a battlefield, waged between the id (our basic instincts), the ego (our rational selves), and the superego (our moral compass). When a person gains power, it's as if they've tilted this balance—not unlike an overeager kid on a seesaw—towards the id, creating a tug-of-war between our unchecked instincts and our rational, ethical selves. After all, with power comes privilege, and with privilege comes freedom from many of the constraints that bind regular folks.

Often, individuals in positions of power can begin to feel invincible. Studies have suggested that those with power are more likely to take financial risks, make quick and impulsive decisions, and have higher levels of testosterone, which can result in increased aggression and decreased empathy. But at the same time, power can also lead to positive changes. It can bolster self-confidence, prompt people to take responsibility, and even make them more honest in some cases.

The key to understanding how power changes people lies in the concept of "power distance". Power distance is essentially how much a person is willing to accept the social distance that exists between those with power and those without. When there is a high power distance, individuals are more likely to defer to authority and less likely to challenge the status quo. This can create a fertile breeding ground for autocratic and paternalistic styles of leadership – styles that are less about serving the public and more about consolidating personal power.

On the other hand, individuals who perceive a lower power distance are less tolerant of authority. They are likely to challenge their superiors, negotiate their role and fight for their rights. This recognizes power as not merely something that a person has, but something that a person does. It posits that power is not a static entity, but an active and dynamic process that is affirmed and redefined through every interaction we have.

The danger, naturally, lies in power's potential for abuse. The infamous Stanford Prison Experiment by psychologist Philip Zimbardo demonstrated just how perilous unchecked power can be. Given authority over pretend "prisoners", the experiment's "guards" fell too easily into their roles, growing increasingly sadistic as the experiment went on.

Zimbardo's experiment challenges us to reflect on the institutions we build and the cultures we cultivate. How do we prevent power from corrupting those who wield it? Is it a question of better checks and balances? Stronger accountability measures? Or perhaps, as some might suggest, the solution lies in fostering a culture that prizes cooperation over competition, compassion over conquest.

But perhaps the greatest transformation power brings is the one that occurs within. Absolute power not only corrupts absolutely, as the saying goes, but it can also isolate absolutely. Consider the mob boss, who has to live in constant worry of betrayal from his underlings, or the despotic ruler, who becomes paranoid and suspicious, trusting no one—not even themselves.

Therefore, we come to see how power is not simply a lever one pulls or a button one pushes—it is a profound psychological state with far-reaching consequences. It is a force that shapes who we are, how we think, and how we behave.

Understanding the relationship between power and psychology is crucial in tackling issues of governance, justice, and inequality. We must delve deep into the power dynamics embedded in our culture, our politics, and indeed, our everyday relationships. Acknowledging the profound ways in which power transforms people and relationships is a critical step towards fostering societies that are not just powerful, but also compassionate, equitable, and just.

In essence, the psychology of power and how it alters individuals not only shapes societies, but the narratives we tell and how we understand our own personal stories. It is pervasive, complex, but also meticulously reliant on our own human instincts, desires and fears.

Perhaps the final thought to consider is that power, being so integral to the human experience, cannot be evaded or ignored. Rather, it must be negotiated with, navigated through and ultimately understood for us to harness its potential for the collective good of society. After all, power in the right hands can be a vehicle of positive change and a driver of progress.

Chapter 2:
The Types of Crimes

Segueing from our analysis of the allure of power, we now delve into the potential symptoms of its misuse: the types of crimes. The spectrum of crimes that can involve individuals in positions of influence is as vast as a desert night sky—illuminated by occasional horrifying acts of indiscretion. Beginning at the monetary end, we encounter bribery and embezzlement—two prolific instances of financial crimes—where profit rather than the public good becomes the central motive for a leader's actions. Then, there's the abuse of power—nefarious deeds marked by coercion, nepotism, manipulation, which exemplify the ugliness that unregulated power can breed. It's like a domino effect that topples into moral failings of personal indiscretions and scandals that expose the frail human behind the facade. Some crimes escalate to the seriousness of 'high crimes'—treason, espionage, and other severe offenses —that shake the very groundwork of the nation. From conspiracy to defraud the United States, obstructing official proceedings, violating the Racketeer Influenced and Corrupt Organizations Act, to solicitation of violation of oath by public officer—each of these offenses signifies a profound betrayal against the nation that trusted these leaders with power. And not to forget, the relatively less dramatic but just as damaging crimes of forgery, filing false documents, making false statements and withholding vital national defense information. Each crime represents a distinct facet of the complexities of corruption that unfortunately plague our political landscape. The harsh reality is, some people can't handle the responsibility that accompanies power and allow their personal ambitions to taint their public responsibilities.

Financial Crimes: Bribery, Embezzlement, and Beyond

Entering the dim labyrinths of the financial underworld, we encounter the murky realm of bribery, embezzlement, and other financial crimes. These are acts committed by individuals and organizations whom greed and lust for power have led astray. In this section, we'll attempt to shed light on these transgressions.

At first blush, bribery might seem fairly straightforward—a greased palm, a covert nod, a discreet handover of an envelop. But this is not always the case. In its broadest sense, bribery involves giving or receiving anything of value to influence the actions of another party. Not limited to raw cash, it can take the form of gifts, tickets, holidays, or even loans with favorable terms. It's a dangerous dance of favors and expectations, a crime hidden behind acts of ostensible generosity.

The harm inflicted by bribery is multifaceted. It undermines trust, tarnishes reputations, and degrades the ethical fabric of society. Also, it often exacerbates wealth disparity since those who bribe their way often dispose of an unwarranted advantage. It's like jumping the queue in a vast supermarket that is society.

As we go down the rabbit hole, let's ponder at another financial crime—embezzlement. When we think of theft, we may conjure images of burglars or pickpockets. Embezzlement, though, is a more insidious form of theft. It involves the misapplication of funds entrusted to someone's care for their own use or advantage.

Unlike regular theft, embezzlement often involves a betrayal of trust. The embezzler could be a trusted employee, a family member, a financial advisor, or, at times, a public official. These are people riding on a wave of trust until that trust capsizes under the weight of their illicit actions.

Fundamentally, embezzlement involves three components—the fraudulent conversion of funds, the resources are entrusted to the care of the embezzler, and the embezzler's intention to wrongfully use the funds. It's like a magic trick where the hand is faster than the eye, and before you know it, the money is gone.

Resource diversion, payroll fraud, and fraudulent loans are examples of embezzlement. This deceptively simple crime can combust a business, wreak havoc on public trust, and compromise the most solid of reputations.

But financial crime is not limited to bribery and embezzlement, oh no, it's an umbrella term that covers a vast landscape of illegal activities. Inside this umbrella, we also find crimes like falsifying business records.

Falsifying records is an act of deception. It involves changing, modifying, or tampering with a document with the intention to deceive. This can range from inflating expense accounts, to understating income on a tax return, or altering inventory records to hide theft.

What makes falsifying business records particularly worrisome is the cascading effect of misinformation that it leads to. It can skew market behavior, mislead investors, or even precipitate the decline of a company. Once the whistle is blown, the dominoes start to fall, causing losses and damaging credibility.

Who can forget the infamous Enron scandal where Enron's top executives conspired to hide debt and inflate profits? Here the corporate behemoth's collapse was concrete evidence of the severe damage that falsifying business records can inflict.

Each of these financial crimes, whether it be bribery, embezzlement, or falsifying records, has a common thread running through them. Each is characterized by deceit, concealment, and violation of trust. They are veiled activities hidden from the public eye and often facilitated by a web of convoluted transactions.

The consequences of these financial crimes ripple through society, eroding trust, undermining institutions, and damaging economies. Not Measuring these costs solely in terms of dollars and cents is criminally simplistic. Instead, look at it through the lens of trust and societal integrity; here, the true cost of these crimes come to light.

Peeling back the layers of financial crimes allows us an opportunity to confront the truth and seek lessons in these tales of misdeeds. By understanding these crimes' modus operandi, we not only equip ourselves with knowledge but also instigate change towards establishing a society more resistant to such crimes. After all, being forewarned is being forearmed.

As we traverse deeper into the following chapters, we'll explore how detection, punishment, and prevention mechanisms strengthen social fabric against these acts. Because, while we can't prevent the greed that often fuels financial crimes, we can strive to make sure it doesn't pay off.

Abuse of Power: Coercion, Nepotism, and Manipulation

Power is a significant element in the realm of politics, often acting as a double-edged sword. When used appropriately, it can effect positive change in communities, states, and even on a national level. However, when used inappropriately, it can lead to egregious acts that jeopardize the essence of democracy. This segment examines the abuse of power through coercion, nepotism, and manipulation.

Coercion is an overt exertion of power where a person leverages their power to force another person to act contrary to their wishes. In politics, coercion manifests in various ways, such as coercion by threat or by force. It's not uncommon to hear stories about political leaders using their power and influence to suppress critics, force adherence to a certain course of action, or even drive opponents out of the political arena. This behavior tears at the fabric of democratic societies and undermines the principle of free and fair competition, which is a cornerstone of democracy.

Coercion also rears its head in the form of economic and political blackmail. This conduct often involves threats to cut off resources or support unless certain conditions are met. While seemingly less violent, this form of coercion can be just as harmful and significantly disrupt the lives and livelihoods of the individuals involved.

Worse yet, state resources can often be mobilized, in graver cases of coercion, to surveil, intimidate, or even detain individuals. The use of law enforcement agencies or intelligence entities to unjustly pressure or influence individuals is not unheard of, further highlighting the dangerous potential of unchecked power.

On the other hand, nepotism involves favoring family members and friends, often at the expense of merit or the collective interest of the electorate. This practice detracts from the preeminence of competence and credibility in government appointment. It perpetuates dynastic rule, erodes public trust, and stifens diversity and fresh perspectives—something that is vital for any thriving society.

Nepotism also negates the importance of equal opportunities and inclusive decision-making. It discourages those without political connections, curbing social mobility and exacerbating socio-economic disparities. Besides, it can breed inefficiencies from the infiltration of inexperienced or underqualified individuals into positions of power.

Manipulation introduces another form of power misuse. This frequently involves deception or distortion of information to sway public perception or induce certain actions. Leaders may wield their influence to manipulate legislation, misrepresent facts, or suppress vital information, effectively skewing democratic proceedings.

Propaganda has historically been a tool of manipulation, with politicians utilizing media outlets, speeches, or social platforms to place their narratives in the most favorable light. This circumvents the public's ability to make informed decisions, causing short and long-term negative outcomes.

Furthermore, manipulation can extend to uses of power that incite fear, stoke divisiveness, or propagate falsehoods. These actions undermine social cohesion, amplify civic unrest, and threaten the unity which is fundamental to a functioning society.

While coercion, nepotism, and manipulation are distinct, they are inextricably linked. They signal an abuse of power, tarnishing the office those leaders occupy and eroding public faith in government institutions. Any of these practices betray those in the shadows of power: the everyday citizen.

The durability of a democratic system depends upon the strength of its institutions and its leaders' commitment to upholding standards of fairness and integrity. Recognizing and understanding these forms of power abuse is the first step towards demanding greater accountability from our politicians, confronting these issues head-on, and preserving our democracy.

The integrity of public office calls for ethical leadership, respect for the rule of law, and a commitment to public service. The lack of any of these qualities can pave the way for coercion, nepotism, and manipulation, highlighting the importance of voting in leaders who display these attributes.

As we proceed, let's dive deeper into the dreadful consequences of these forms of power abuse, looking at the mechanisms which enable them and the safeguards necessary to combat them. We cannot afford to be passive spectators of the politics, only active participants can effect the change we seek. Our democratic fabric depends on each of us learning, recognizing, and calling out these abuses of power when they occur.

Moral Failings: Scandals and Personal Indiscretions

When a public leader is found to be embroiled in a scandal, it's a sobering reminder that no one, regardless of their position, is free of human potential for mistake or ego-driven behavior. It also underscores the complex interaction between individual ethics and systemic structures, revealing the darker side of political life: moral failings.

Let's focus our lens on one of the most prevalent types of these failings: personal indiscretions. Often these are propelled into the public eye, shattering the images carefully curated by the politicians or public figures in question. Whether it's marital unfaithfulness, undisclosed addictions, or other disreputable behavior, the personal indiscretions of our leaders risk undermining their authority and the public trust they hold.

A prime example of marital infidelity turned scandal is the Monica Lewinsky saga in the Bill Clinton administration. This scandal was sensational, not only for the immorality at play but for the perjury that followed. Similar tales punctuate American political history, not restricted to any party or ideology.

However, it's important to distinguish between personal moral failings and illegal activities. Not all personal indiscretions are criminal but they often carry significant political consequences. These may include resignations, terminations, or sizable drops in the polls. The effects can be long-lasting, often overshadowing a politician's accomplishments.

What worries many observers are the underlying patterns these scandals highlight. Do we elect leaders with certain personality traits more likely to give in to temptation? Or does the culture of power and privilege create an environment where such behavior is more probable than elsewhere?

Evidence from psychology and sociology suggests it might be a bit of both. Research indicates that people, in positions of power, can become detached from the societal norms that guide typical behavior. This detachment can cultivate an environment where indiscretions seem less significant, less real, or even justified.

Another facet of personal indiscretions widely broadcasted in headlines is substance abuse. In the recent past, public officials have been caught in scandals surrounding drug and alcohol abuse. Such personal failings present an uncomfortable dichotomy. The public figure is burdened with their struggle, often played out in the public sphere, whereas their political persona suffers a severe hit. Despite the social stigma around addiction reducing with time and more understanding around it as a medical condition, in politics, it remains a significant scandal.

But, dispositional weaknesses do not account for all instances of personal indiscretions. Some situations hint at broader systemic issues. Sexual harassment and assault allegations, for example, have led to high-profile resignations and dismissals, highlighting a culture of misogyny and power abuse present in many political structures.

The #MeToo movement, born out of Hollywood, found echoes within the halls of Capitol Hill as well, as women broke their silence on sexual misconduct by powerful political figures. This episode demonstrated that even in the 21st century, many governmental structures still tolerate, or at least overlook, sexual misconduct.

Knee-deep in the digital age, indiscretions also extend to cyberspace. Leaders have found themselves caught in controversies involving inappropriate messages, email mishandlings, and disreputable online activity. Accessibility to digital communication platforms has not just led to increased transparency but also made personal indiscretions easier to commit and harder to hide.

Personal indiscretions, thus, represent a complex interplay of individual weaknesses, systemic failures, and societal pressures. Such transgressions stand to erode public trust, render leaders unelectable, and, sometimes, lead to legal repercussions. Arguably, no political career is worth the loss of personal integrity and the harm caused to affected individuals.

The solution to most of these failings seem simple in principle, yet complex in practice. Society's call for leaders of moral and ethical strength is audible, and the hope is for leaders themselves to answer that call. Parties and political organizations also need to work towards nurturing a culture of integrity and accountability.

As we contemplate on these moral failings, we should not forget to look inwards. After all, politicians are a reflection of the society that elects them. It gives us an opportunity to reassess our own moral compass, and demand better of those we entrust with our representation.

High Crimes: Treason, Espionage, and Other Severe Offenses

Wading deeper into the murky waters of political transgressions, we now turn our attention to high crimes. These are offenses of an extremely severe nature—so grave, in fact, that the United States Constitution explicitly defines them as grounds for impeachment. The most notorious of these are treason and espionage, chilling words that evoke images of spies, double agents, and Benedict Arnolds. Treason is defined as levying war against the U.S. or aiding its enemies, a cardinal betrayal of national trust. Espionage constitutes spying and unlawful trading of secrets, potentially endangering encompassing national security. But the realm of high crimes extends beyond just these two. It spans to a multitude of offenses, encompassing everything from conspiracy to defraud the United States to obstructing an official proceeding. There's also falsely impersonating a public officer or willfully retaining national defense information, violating the Espionage Act. It's important to realize the gravity of these offenses, as they represent not just deliberate violations of the law or ethics, but profound betrayals of the public trust. Understanding them takes us one step closer to comprehending the vast spectrum of corruption.

Treason, as we delve into the realm of high crimes within American politics, demands special attention. Often conjured bleakly in history books or sensationalized in espionage films, treason exists as the most severe offense against one's own nation. The United States Constitution keeps it distinctly confined to times of war, with a clear definition stating that, "Treason against the United States, shall consist only in levying War against them, or in adhering to their Enemies, giving them Aid and Comfort." The severity of this crime is underpinned not just by its direct transgression against the state, but by the profound betrayal it entails.

The rare nature of treason, as well as its severe penalties, can at times shroud the crime in a mist of uncertainty or disbelief, and yet it remains an undeniable element of political malfeasance. Notably, the conviction of treason requires "two Witnesses to the same overt Act, or on Confession in open Court," a high bar set to prevent the misuse of such an impactful charge. This reflects the gravity with which treason is regarded, demonstrating a balance struck to guard against both the transgressor and a misuse of the accusation.

Historically, acts of treason have been incredibly rare, with fewer than 30 formal charges of treason leveled in over two hundred years of American history. Yet these instances come steeped in a chilling sense of drama, often intimately intertwined with turbulent periods of conflict, war, and social division. From the notorious case of Julius and Ethel Rosenberg, who were executed for selling atomic secrets to the Soviet Union during the Cold War, to the less-known case of Walter Allen, a Civil War era politician who attempted to aid the Confederate rebellion, each episode carries distinct lessons about loyalty, power, and the perils of betrayal. Underscoring these lessons is the sobering realization that even in a democratic society guided by principles of justice and freedom, the specter of treason can emerge from the shadows, presenting a stern challenge to these revered principles.

Espionage, often cloaked with mystery in movies and literature, is a far grimmer entity in reality, particularly when it snakes its way into the vast and complex structure of American politics. On the surface, public servants are entrusted with leading the nation, making policies, and ensuring the overall well-being of the citizens. However, underneath this noble exterior, there are individuals who can be lured by the seduction of power, not for the betterment of their constituents, but for self-gain or the interests of another sovereign power. Espionage, in this context, is incredibly dangerous, as it usually involves the transmission of highly sensitive, classified information affecting national security to foreign bodies.

The penetrating gaze and vast reach of espionage are not limited to spy novels and clandestine agencies. Supreme Court Justice Hugo Black once wrote, "In plain English, spy means peeking, and peeking, generally speaking, is not a dignified business." Rather, its roots can embed themselves into the most unlikely, yet influential areas of the political landscape. It doesn't always involve the image of a trench-coated spy carrying out surreptitious operations; modern-day espionage could be as simple as using technology to steal confidential data remotely, or exerting influence from within the government to sway policies and decisions. Yet the consequences of such acts can be far-reaching, jeopardizing not only individual lives but the soul of the nation itself.

Consider this - a politician or public servant, whether out of greed, unsatiated ambition, or coercion, becomes a mole within American corridors of power. Such a person gains access to information that could affect millions of lives. This information, when shared with unfriendly foreign powers or agencies, could compromise national security, endanger American interests at home and abroad, and erode the very foundations of the democratic fabric. Espionage brings a whole new level of severity to the realm of high crimes, and once unveiled, it can shatter the public's trust in their leaders and the system at large, with reverberating effects for years to come.

Conspiracy to defraud the United States baffles many because of its broad implications and the understandable confusion around exactly what the term means. In a nutshell, this crime pertains to any calculated action taken with the intention of cheating the government— and by extension, the American people—of things of value or obstructing lawful governmental functions. The key here is that it doesn't necessarily require an element of deception or monetary fraud, as one might initially surmise.

We can better comprehend this by looking at some notable cases. Take as an example, a political campaign knowingly accepting foreign interference to influence voters' perception of a candidate. This is generally conceived as a conspiracy due to the aim of undermining trust in the election process, which is a lawful function of the government. It's a complex realm, where the line between acceptable behavior and criminal activity can sometimes appear blurred.

In the pursuit of justice, challenges arise from the very nature of this crime. Due to its broad definition, prosecution could potentially be used as a political weapon. On the other hand, constraining definitions may allow for corrupt behavior to slip through the cracks, unquestioned. Maintaining balance is key, and it's in this nuanced gray zone that we can find a fascinating reflection of our nation's struggle to uphold integrity within its political sphere, while safeguarding against potential abuses of power. The health of our democracy depends, in large part, on how meticulously we examine, understand, and address issues such as these.

Obstructing an Official Proceeding – it sounds like a nebulous term, doesn't it? But in reality, it's a highly serious legal infraction. At its root, this crime involves intentionally hindering, postponing, or interfering with governmental operations. These operations are not limited to judicial hearings; they may also span Congressional proceedings, Federal agency operations, or even investigations within the Department of Justice. The aim is simple: to interrupt the natural and lawful execution of an official action.

Think of obstructing an official proceeding like throwing a wrench into the gears of a well-oiled machine. It's an attempt to disrupt the smooth and efficient function of government, often with an intention to favor one's own interests or escape accountability. For instance, if someone were to destroy documents, lie under oath, or intimidate witnesses to thwart an investigation or legal process, they would be committing this crime. It's the power equivalent of tossing a smoke bomb on the floor to create a diversion; a high stakes game that puts self-interest ahead of national welfare.

Obstruction cuts to the heart of justice, undermining the integrity of our democratic systems. It contributes to the erosion of public trust in our institutions, and the implications are not taken lightly by the courts. If found guilty, violators can face severe penalties including imprisonment and hefty fines. Remember that power's allure can lead some down a dangerous path, and obstructing an official proceeding is a hard, tangible example of that slippery slope. It's also a clear reminder of why checks and balances exist, and why vigilant citizens are crucial in holding our public servants accountable.

Conspiracy Against Rights takes the abuse of power to a new level. It's not an isolated act of corruption or personal indiscretion. Instead, it's a calculated, well-orchestrated plot designed to blatantly or subtly undermine and bypass the rights of citizens. For public officers entrusted with safeguarding our nation's principles, this deception represents a flagrant betrayal of the public's trust and their oath to uphold the constitution.

The notion of conspiracy against rights is firmly rooted in 18 U.S.C. § 241 of our United States Code. This specific statute protects individuals against anyone -- often conspirators working in unison -- who attempts to "injure, oppress, threaten, or intimidate" anyone in the enjoyment of any right secured by the Constitution or laws of the United States. And yet, the tragic reality is that those we elect and appoint to public office aren't always exempt from such offenses. Amid the intoxication of power, some choose to conspire against and impede the very rights they vowed to protect.

So, how does such a conspiracy manifest itself? While it may not always involve cloaks and daggers, its execution can be no less deadly to the principles of our democracy. It might begin with the passing of controversial legislation under secretive, non-democratic processes, or perhaps through willful obstruction and stonewalling of investigations, a form of decision-making that jeopardizes our system of checks and balances. It could also involve the intentional manipulation of electoral processes or districts to skew results, a tactic known as gerrymandering. In its more extreme forms, this conspiracy might infiltrate the judicial system, corrupting the sanctuary of justice and fair adjudication. Regardless of the specific method, the endgame remains consistent: to restrict, suppress, or manipulate rights secured by our Constitution, thus undercutting the very essence of democracy.

Violating the Racketeer Influenced and Corrupt Organizations Act is no child's play. When you think of racketeering, your mind might jump to scenes in old, noir-inspired movies featuring notorious gangsters running underground gambling or illicit alcohol rings. But, here's a small correction: it's not exclusively the stuff of Al Capone anymore. Modern versions of racketeering often weave their way through the highest tiers of government, obscured by the intricate complexities of bureaucracy. The Racketeer Influenced and Corrupt Organizations Act, or RICO, is a federal law designed to combat such organized crime.

In the political arena, RICO violations look a little different. They'll probably involve political operatives orchestrating kickback schemes or manipulating government contracts, among other corrupt ventures. It might even be as deep as a group of public officials working in cahoots to manipulate the system for their own ends. The underlying drive remains the same: power and profit. Violating RICO is a serious charge. Because criminal organizations are frequently involved in multiple kinds of illicit activities, the penalties for RICO convictions can be grave. Indeed, the specter of RICO looms large, casting a long and threatening shadow over the offices where public officials once felt invincible.

The thing to remember is this: RICO isn't exactly an easy charge to prove. There needs to be clear evidence of the ongoing, organized nature of the criminal activity. It requires building a concrete case of a pattern of racketeering related to an enterprise's operations—not a standalone act of corruption. An important element here is the definition of "enterprise"—which can include political offices or even an entire governmental agency. So, it's less about proving a solo act of bribery or a singular instance of contracts-fixing, and more about unravelling an intricate web of ongoing organized crime stretching its tendrils across the folds of the political landscape.

Solicitation of Violation of Oath by Public Officer delves into the scenario in which a public officer, driven by the intoxicating cocktail of ambition and potential gain, actively encourages another to betray their official oath. Tricky to detect and fraught with peril, this offense is riddled with legal and ethical implications. It is a masterclass in manipulation, a cruel dance where the stakes are far too high.

At the heart of this violation is a provocative concept - can one be held responsible for the actions of others? In the context of this crime, the answer is a resounding 'yes.' If a public officer, someone entrusted with upholding the law, resorts to enticing others to break their solemn oath, this act constitutes a significant breach of trust. But who pays the price, and how is it calculated? The violation is measured not only by the act itself but by the irreparable damage it inflicts on the foundation of our civil society.

The intricacy of this crime makes it particularly challenging to prove. Prosecutors are tasked with proving intent - a notoriously elusive concept. Were the actions of the public officer in question fueled by a calculated attempt to prompt a violation of trust? Or does the situation merely reflect unfortunate circumstances misinterpreted? The legality and ethics of solicitation of violation of oath by a public officer, an area fraught with grey areas, invite passionate debate and careful scrutiny. Sometimes, the very structures designed to protect us can, in the hands of those with dubious intentions, become weapons of inadvertent havoc. It indeed puts into perspective the delicate balance of power and responsibility in positions of public trust.

Conspiracy to Commit Impersonating a Public Officer is among the less discussed yet incredibly damaging forms of misconduct that can occur within the realm of political crime. At its core, this crime involves an individual or group of individuals intentionally taking on the identity of a public servant with the purpose of achieving certain illegal or unethical advantages. Whether for personal gain or to progress a more comprehensive illicit agenda, these actions can deeply undermine the principles of public trust and democratic legitimacy.

Frequently, conspiracy to impersonate a public officer is linked with other types of crimes such as fraud, corruption, blackmail, or manipulation. The orchestrators may employ complex schemes -- inventing fake emergencies, for instance, or leveraging the assumed authority of their false personas to deceive the public or specific individuals. While the impersonated public servants themselves are victims of sorts, the primary victims are the unsuspecting citizens who trust in the reliability and integrity of their public institutions.

A significant challenge in eradicating this crime lies in its detection. Often, the criminals behind these acts are sufficiently skilled in duplicating the mannerisms, language, and even appearance of the public officials they impersonate, making them hard to distinguish from the genuine article. Furthermore, the digital age has granted these imposters greater opportunity to exploit technological tools and social media platforms to spread disinformation and orchestrate their fraudulent agendas. It's important to note this isn't just a local or state-level issue; the ramifications of these actions can seep into national politics, potentially jeopardizing the stability of our entire democracy. Recognizing the severity of this crime is crucial, as is bolstering efforts towards prevention and penalizing these ill deed's architects.

Conspiracy to Commit Forgery in the First Degree is a crime that doesn't often make headlines, yet it frequents the underbelly of political challenges. It's not as glamorous as treason or as direct as bribery, but forgery, particularly when involving a co-conspirator or two, is a weapon within the arsenal of many political villains. This crime refers to the intention to deceive, through the unauthorized creation or alteration of a document, with the intent of causing damage or receiving some form of illicit gain. Remember, its not the act of forgery, but the intent of conspiring to commit the act, which magnify the criminality within the political sphere.

Acknowledging the question as to why one might conspire to commit such an act, the motivations vary. They range from falsifying voter registration records, manipulating financial certificates, to corrupting legal certificates, and so forth. It's a crime that thrives in the shadows, hidden behind red tape and bureaucratic barriers, and often, it's inseparable from other layers of corruption. For instance, another politician might be looped in as a co-conspirator, or an innocent third party may be manipulated for the act, thus pushing the forgery into the realm of coercion or abuse of power. It's a multifaceted crime, the effects of which ripple through the system, infecting various levels of infrastructure.

While the intricacies of Conspiracy to Commit Forgery in the First Degree are complex, there are controls in place to catch such acts. These checks and balances rely heavily on two factors: Individuals with a keen eye for detail and an incorruptible commitment to transparency, and a prosecutorial system that is both assertive and fair. Still, as with any crime, the best method of control is prevention. That said, understanding the nuances of this crime is the first step towards reckoning with its existence and working towards solutions that aim to dismantle the space it occupies in our political landscape.

False Statements and Writings form a distinctive category within the scope of political infractions. Here, individuals engage in the act of falsifying personal or public records with malicious intent or for personal gain. The action itself may seem innocuous, but the ripple effects can be devastating and far-reaching, impinging on the credibility of government institutions, compromising public trust, or even shifting the trajectories of key policies and decisions.

Imagine if, let's say, a city mayor intentionally misrepresents his city's crime rates to attract investors and developers for a massive urban development project. He produces falsified reports, touting a decrease in crime rates, when the truth is quite the opposite. Surely, these investors and developers, swayed by the reports, may pump money into the project, anticipating great returns. Soon, the spurious project is underway, altering the cityscape and potentially destabilizing the area's socio-economic fabric. It certainly highlights just how damaging and deceptive these false statements and writings can be. Misinformation isn't happening in a vacuum but impacts real lives and communities negatively.

Furthermore, making false statements and writings can contour the political landscape, clouding the truth, and perpetuating deceit. It can manifest as anything from a white lie about a politician's credentials to convince voters, to a false account presented under oath during a high-stakes investigation or trial. These acts muddy the waters of public discourse, tainting our understanding of truth and veracity. Consequently, it has dire implications for governance and democratic representation. It's crucial that we remember this, possessing the knowledge to distinguish fact from fiction, and the wisdom to demand transparency and veracity from our leaders.

Filing False Documents carries shades of sly cunning or blatant disregard for law and truth. In the context of public officials, it can frame them as actors in a thriller, slipping falsified papers into a stack of legitimate ones to serve an ulterior motive. But let's scratch the cinematic surface and focus on the nitty-gritty details.

Breaking down the concept, we encounter two actions: Filing, which simply refers to the process of officially submitting documents to a government or legal entity, and "False", bringing in the deceit factor. This encompasses the creating, altering, or presenting of documents with intentionally misleading or fraudulent information. As mundane as filing papers might sound, the addition of "false" ramps up the potential danger exponentially. If our public officials are complicit in such behaviors, it chips away at the very foundation of our trust based societal structure.

The reasons behind this kind of dishonesty can range from concealing illegal activities, intentionally misleading investigations, or even efforts to defraud ordinary citizens. Regardless of the motivation, the action of filing false documents is a stain on the fabric of any functioning democracy. It tends to trickle down, sowing distrust and discontent among the public, stirring questions about the integrity of our leaders, and eventually undermining our entire political system. As citizens, our vigilance is paramount in ensuring each paper put into the system is as truthful as the democratic values we hold dear.

Willful Retention of National Defense Information in Violation of the Espionage Act is a particularly evocative charge, one that suggests a weighty betrayal of trust and a disregard for national security. At its core, this offense involves the deliberate withholding of information pertaining to national defense from those entitled to receive it, often to the detriment of the nation. This violation isn't just limited to spies surreptitiously passing secrets to foreign entities — it can also include public officials who refuse to relinquish or purposefully retain secret information that they no longer have a legitimate purpose to access.

This charge is addressed under the Espionage Act of 1917, a federal law intended to prevent the support of United States enemies during wartime. In the name of patriots and protectors of the nation, it unfortunately doesn't take a sell-out mission to a foreign body to run afoul of this legislation. Even the mishandling of classified documents, without any expressed intent of betrayal, can drag someone into legal trouble. What's more, those implicated need not be James Bond-esque figures skulking in the shadows, big names in politics, or senior government officials too — have tripped over this legal pitfall.

The severity of an infringement depends on the type, amount, and sensitivity of the information involved, as well as the potential damage to the United States' national security. It's serious business, sanctioned with penalties that can include lengthy prison sentences and hefty fines. When it comes to the Espionage Act, ignorance isn't an excuse under the law. So, whether it's a covert operation straight out of a spy thriller or a case of irresponsible handling of classified documents, it's critical for those with access to national defense information to handle with great care, less they stumble into the sticky territory of willful retention in violation of the Espionage Act. Besides, aren't we all meant to be team players in the larger game of national security?

Chapter 3: The Mechanisms of Corruption

Pausing on the front steps of our exploration into the haunting mansion of corruption, let's now arm ourselves with a torch to illuminate its complex machinery. It's crucial to understand that corruption isn't a spontaneous event, but a system, fueled by seemingly innocuous practices ingrained in our political landscape. Take lobbyists, for instance, who are often seen as benevolent agents providing lawmakers with insights into diverse issues. Yet, alarmingly, their significant financial backing can *buy influence*, effectively making our representatives beholden to their sponsors' wishes rather than the public interest. Next is the seductive dance of campaign finance. While it appears as an inevitable part of any political campaign, this system is riddled with slippery slopes. Exorbitant donations from powerful corporations or wealthy individuals can transmute into a perverse quid pro quo relationship, with policymaking the commodity up for sale. Lastly, let's not ignore the old power play of patronage; favoritism has evolved into an art form in our corridors of power. High-ranking officials dole out important positions to their friends and allies, compromising meritocracy and fostering an ecosystem prime for corruption. All of these factors interconnect, coalescing into a mechanism that greases the wheels of this nefarious machinery.

The Role of Lobbyists: Influence for Sale

On the surface, lobbyists appear as legitimate professionals in tailor-made suits, possessing powers of persuasion instrumental in shaping American policy. They operate in the bustling corridors of Washington D.C., maintaining a constant presence either behind closed doors or on the House and Senate floors. A more incisive look, however, reveals a nuanced portrayal, shrouded in both ambiguity and controversy.

Lobbying is legal. It is constitutionally protected under the First Amendment, assuring the right of citizens to petition their government. Herein, however, lies a problematic loophole. Because lobbyists serve as intermediaries between interest groups and lawmakers, they possess an undue voice in shaping legislation. They're essentially salespeople who peddle influence rather than products, swapping big money for big favors.

The principle behind lobbying is straight from a high school Civics class: in a democracy, individuals and groups have the right (and in some cases, the responsibility) to voice their concerns to their representatives. The intention here is to inform and sway the lawmakers' decisions on consequential matters to better represent their constituents.

But, like the rules in a high school classroom, the principle can easily be bent or broken. Therein lies the danger. The exchange of information can easily be distorted into a conduit for manipulation, a position that lobbying, due to its unique and intimate access to lawmakers, often straddles. The benevolent "educator" can rapidly morph into the cunning manipulator.

The best lobbyists possess a deft understanding of the legislative process, sharp interpersonal skills, and connections to lawmakers. However, a lobbyist's most powerful tool is the financial muscle. This wealth, whether contributed directly to campaigns or expended on advocacy and persuasion efforts, can flex significant influence on the legislative outcomes.

Lobbyists often represent deep-pocketed entities: business conglomerates, influential industries, labor unions, and non-profit organizations, all of whom have a vested interest in swaying legislation. Thus, money becomes a critical factor, giving these entities an uneven playing field and magnifying their voices above those of the average citizen.

What's more, lobbying is often an inside job. Consider the 'revolving door' phenomena where ex-politicians slip effortlessly into roles as lobbyists. Armed with contacts and keen insights into the workings of government, these former public servants make potent allies for interest groups. Their intimate knowledge of the intricacies of the legislative process, coupled with their former colleague connections in still in office, makes them the ultimate power players in lobbying.

However, there is a subtler side to this narrative. Many lobbyists genuinely believe they are advocating for commendable causes. An environmental lobbyist pushing for cleaner air, a healthcare lobbyist advocating for better patient policies, or an education lobbyist striving for higher funding, all operate under the mantra of public interest. But it's the insertion of money into the equation that cloud the line between public advocacy and special interest pandering.

While there is a growing consensus that lobbying needs reform, ideas about what those reforms should look like are far from unified. Proposals range from stricter limits on campaign donations to reforms aimed at reducing the symbiotic relationship between lobbyists and lawmakers, legislation that forces more transparency, and potential tax incentives to encourage 'small-dollar' lobbying.

Still, the lobbyist's ability to navigate complex legislative waters and the scope of their influence keep them entrenched in the system. Even if incremental steps towards reform succeed, the road ahead is long, winding, and fraught with resistance.

Therefore, understanding the role of lobbyists in our democratic process leads to broader questions about the health and vitality of our democracy. Can we truly lay claim to the ideal of 'government by the people' when money, power, and influence are such critical determinants of policy outcomes?

Whilst implicit lobbying tactics remain a thorny issue in our political landscape, it will require robust, comprehensive, and daring reform measures to curb their broader effects, replacing the 'governing by the loudest' paradigm with one that upholds the basics of a representative democracy.

Only then can we prevent the commodification of our democracy and ensure that lawmakers remain true to their duty: serving their constituents and not simply the highest bidder. Conclusively, vacating the haunting specter of the influence-for-sale phenomenon and championing instead a democracy truly for the people, not just the privileged few.

Campaign Finance: A Slippery Slope

Our journey into the mechanisms of corruption in American politics brings us to an ever topical issue - campaign finance. Arguably, this is where the rubber meets the road, where ambitions either soar or come crashing down. It's the key that opens the door to power, but it is also the bait that leads many civic-minded individuals down a slippery slope to potential corruption.

Let's start by considering what campaign finance actually involves. In essence, it is the funding that helps candidates run their election campaigns. Think billboards, radio ads, televised debates, staff salaries, travel expenses, and all the other logistics of getting a candidate into office, and you begin to see the astronomical costs involved. Here's where it starts to get tricky - where does this money come from?

In theory, financial support comes from individuals, organizations, political action committees (PACs), and the candidates' own pockets. However, as the stakes rise and races become more competitive, the monetary demands of successful campaigning often lead candidates into murky waters.

While laws exist to regulate campaign financing, the fact is that these can sometimes be as clear as mud – intentionally or otherwise. This lack of transparent regulations has opened up a host of loopholes that can be exploited by candidates and their supporters.

First, there are limits to how much an individual or organization can directly contribute to a candidate's campaign. However, that's where PACs come in. Born out of a desire to circumvent the contribution caps, these entities can receive and spend unlimited funds on behalf of a candidate, provided they don't coordinate directly with the candidate or their campaign. It sounds like a sensible workaround, in theory.

However, the arrival of Super PACs took things a notch further. They function in much the same way as traditional PACs but with one critical difference – they are allowed to spend their funds expressly advocating for or against a candidate. So, while they may not officially coordinate with a campaign, Super PACs can significantly influence an election's outcome.

The dangers in all this lie in the potential quid pro quo. In an ideal world, these contributions would be made purely out of civic duty. However, it is difficult not to infer that large donations might come with expectations of something in return. This opens the door to a form of legal bribery, fundamentally subverting our democracy.

Perhaps even more concerning is the arrival of 'dark money'. These funds come from organizations that do not have to disclose their donors, which means that large sums of money can find their way into a campaign war chest without the public ever knowing who's behind it.

The Supreme Court decision in Citizens United v. Federal Election Commission (2010) has further compounded these issues. By ruling that government restrictions on independent political spending by corporations and unions violated the First Amendment, the floodgates for corporate money in politics were opened.

These increasingly convoluted loopholes are not just problematic from an ethics standpoint. They also make it difficult for ordinary people to run for office, leading to a situation where only the very wealthy or those with wealthy backers can realistically aspire to a political career.

This is not just about fairness. It impacts the diversity of our political representation and ultimately influences the priorities and decisions of those in power.

Moreover, the system's complexity and lack of transparency also make it difficult for the average voter to make an informed choice. The origins and intentions behind campaign funding can significantly impact how an elected official governs, but unless you're willing to spend hours sleuthing around public records and financial reports, this information can be frustratingly inaccessible.

Yet it needn't be this way. It is entirely possible to create a system that would provide adequate campaign funding without opening the floodgates to potential corruption. It would require constant vigilance, rigorous regulation, and realistic acknowledgment of the realities of electioneering.

In conclusion, campaign finance is a dangerous balancing act – one that highlights the tension between democracy's ideals and the pragmatic realities of politics. It is a slippery slope where one misstep can lead to the violation of regulations, corruption, and the erosion of public trust. It deserves our attention not just during the election season, but also in the quieter moments between elections when these laws are debated, passed, and quietly exploited.

After all, what is at stake here is not just the integrity of individual elections or politicians. It is the very health and trustworthiness of our democratic system – and there could hardly be higher stakes than that.

The Power of Patronage: Friends in High Places

The notion of patronage is as old as politics itself. From the ancient city-states of Greece to the contemporary corridors of power in Washington D.C., much of political history can be read as an ongoing tale of patronage, with its inherent potential for corruption.

Patronage is the act of providing favors, positions, or benefits to loyal supporters; it's the art of you scratch my back, I'll scratch yours. Its power resides in its ability to funnel resources–from jobs to contracts to legislative favors–to allies, bolstering a base of support and consolidating power.

Often, these practices are viewed as a necessary evil; an ill-defined gray area where the act of rewarding loyalty intersects with quid pro quos. This blurry line is what makes patronage so difficult to police and regulate. Often, it is perfectly legal and generally accepted as a routine facet of political life.

The danger of patronage lies not in its legality, but in its potential for misuse. When used indiscriminately, it can breed corruption, engender nepotism, and foster a culture of cronyism. But moreso, it can undermine the very essence of democracy, distorting the balance of power and creating an uneven political landscape where the currency of the realm is favors and connections, not ideas and integrity.

It would be a mistake to believe that patronage is confined to a particular political party or ideology; its roots delve deep into the structure of the political apparatus, spanning the aisles and ideologies. It thrives in the rich soil of political expediency, and it nourishes those who know how to manipulate its powers.

History overflows with tales of the powerful using the currency of patronage to maintain control. The machine politics of Tammany Hall, boss-driven city administrations, and smoke-filled rooms of the last century were all steeped in a culture of rewards and reciprocation. This is an age-old game played out in communities, cities, states, and at the national level.

In modern politics, patronage often takes the form of political appointees. These are the friends, allies, and donors who are rewarded with plum positions in the administration after a successful election. These roles can be as high profile as ambassadorships or as mundane as positions on obscure but influential regulatory boards.

But the exchanges don't stop there. Contracts are another form of political favor. Whether it is construction contracts for infrastructure projects, legal work for government departments, or service contracts for governmental requirements, the allocation of these contracts often reflects political loyalties and connections. In the mired alleyways of corruption, such forms of patronage often border on bribery and kickbacks, opening the door to legal scrutiny and public outrage.

Another type of patronage is legislative favors. Lawmakers often use their positions to benefit friends and allies. Whether through earmarking federal funds for pet projects in their districts or guiding bills that favor their allies through legislature, politicians have a variety of means to reward those who keep them in power.

Patronage can also manifest in less tangible ways, such as providing political cover to allies during scandals or political storms, using one's influence to shield friends from scrutiny or retribution. While this type of patronage is difficult to document or prosecute, it is as old as politics itself and remains a potent tool in the hands of those in power.

It's crucial to contextualize the capital of patronage in the wider realm of power. It's not solely about tit-for-tat exchanges; it's about maintaining power. By rewarding loyalists, a politician bolsters their base, fending off potential rivals and reinforcing their place in the hierarchy.

And yet, while patronage is a hallmark of the system, it's not without its checks and balances. Voters, watchdog groups, and the media can play vital roles in holding public officials accountable for their actions. Even within the political system, there are mechanisms designed to curb the most egregious abuses of power, from ethics committees to anti-corruption laws.

Ultimately, the power of patronage serves as a reminder of the complexities and contradictions inherent in political life. It is a force that can simultaneously hold together and undermine the systems of power, creating a precarious balance that is forever on the brink of disruption.

And so, understanding patronage- its workings, its consequences, and the ways it's checked, is not just about understanding a single aspect of political life. It's about understanding the interplay of power and accountability, loyalty, and corruption. It offers a valuable lens through which we can explore the intricate, frequently messy dynamics that shape our political world.

Chapter 4:
The Judicial Process

As we peel away the layers of the political process, we find ourselves in the riveting realm of the judicial process. At first glance, it might seem next-door-neighbor boring, a mechanical evolution of investigation, indictment, trial, and conviction. But dig deeper, and the picture sharpens to a high-stakes game of chess, where strategy and evidence dance together on a board under the harsh spotlight of public scrutiny. Starting with investigations, our journey nudges open the secretive doors of Grand Jury rooms, where layers of testimonies and exhibits make a compelling case for indictment. We witness the transformation of a public servant into a defendant, a process that unveils the vulnerability of power under the weight of law. The judicial narrative unfolds like a book with each turning page unveiling an new twist—an unexpected defense strategy, a compelling cross-examination, a key piece of evidence. Ultimately, they all boil down to the finale: sentencing. The solemn moment when gavel meets wood, casting a finality of judgment, determining a person's trajectory in one deafening crack. A process instilling fear and respect, the judicial process symbolizes the praxis of democracy by affirmatively stating that no one is above the law.

Investigation and Indictment: The Path to the Courtroom

Following the exploration of types of crimes and mechanisms of corruption that encompass the dark sides of the American political landscape, it is imperative we now venture into the intricacies of the judicial process. Starting with the investigation and indictment stages, let's peel back the curtain on what exactly leads political figures into the harsh glare of the courtroom.

The investigation process is painstakingly thorough, initiated when allegations or strong suspicions arise pointing to a public figure's involvement in criminal activity. It's the time when law enforcement agencies, tasked with the responsibility to uphold the rule of law, focus their resources to find the facts.

A team of specialists from various fields including forensics, IT, law, and finance, is assembled. They work tenaciously poring over records, scrutinizing individuals, and sifting through data. A crucial part of this process involves obtaining and executing search warrants. A search warrant, issued by a judge, provides lawful permission to examine a location or seize evidence linked to the crime being investigated.

Interrogation or interviews often form another key part of this process. While some see it as aggressive and confrontational, an effective interrogation is more of an art than a science - a mix of keen observation, persuasive dialogue, and strategic questioning.

As the facts start to accumulate, so does the tension. The balance of power expected in our democracy is perhaps disrupted, as the role of investigators shifts to liberators of truth. Their findings expose the hidden aspects of power and corruption, often creating shockwaves in the innermost circles of our political sphere.

Once the investigation reaches a certain point and significant evidence is gathered, the case is turned over to a prosecutor. This is where the concept of 'indictment' comes into play.

An indictment is a formal accusation that a person has committed a crime. Grand juries are convened to hear the prosecutor's case. Under the watchful eye of a judge, they review evidence, hear witnesses, and decide whether there's enough to charge a person with a crime.

Remember, indictments are distilled representations of extensive investigations. They explain acts of misconduct and corruption in language that the public can understand and subsequently, hold the accused accountable.

It's worth noting that not all indictments go to trial. Plea bargaining is a common route, where the accused agrees to plead guilty to a lesser charge in return for a lesser sentence.

The delivery of an indictment is a pivotal moment, marking a shift from private investigation to public litigation, when the accused is confronted with their allegations in the courtroom. It is a solemn moment; the start of a process that will either restore or damage their reputation, and potentially change the trajectory of their life substantially.

By this point, these political figures, once untouchable and cloaked in the invincibility of their positions, are thrust into unfamiliar territory, standing equal before the law. It's a sobering return to the fundamental principle that no one is above the law, no matter their rank or status.

Navigating this path to the courtroom is a complex journey that requires patience, diligence and an uncompromised commitment to truth and accountability. The investigation's pressure-cooker atmosphere and the gravity of the indictment set a solemn stage for the upcoming courtroom drama.

Though far from glamorous, these legal processes indeed serve a vital function in the protection of democratic integrity. They facilitate the exposure and prosecution of corruption, reinforcing the boundaries of acceptable conduct for those in positions of power.

Moreover, these processes aptly demonstrate the resilience of a system, where public servants operate under scrutiny, rather than without. However difficult the path may be, the journey towards the courtroom ensures that both power and accountability coexist - one balancing, challenging, and sometimes prosecuting, the other.

The Trial: Public Servant to Defendant

The journey from being a dignitary bathed in limelight, trusted with power, to becoming a rupture in the social fabric, lodged in the dock as a defendant, is a trip down a hellish spiral. Not every public servant embarks on this journey but those who do, face an uphill battle in court, where the public eye watches their every twitch, every facial expression scrutinized, every word cross-examined.

The trial is where the transformation from public servant to defendant is complete. Much like a dramatic metamorphosis, the public servant, once revered, respected, and relied upon, sheds the façade of moral uprightness to confront the consequences of their actions.

The trial phase is crucial in determining the defendant's fate. Here, the charges are explained, evidence is presented, and witnesses are cross-examined. All these elements add to the astonishing spectacle of a high-profile political trial. It is rather interesting to observe this spectacle unfold. A once invincible figure now stands vulnerable, stripped of power and prestige.

The pivot of the trial is the evidence presented by the prosecutors. The gravity and volume of this evidence can alter the pace of the proceeding, shifting the courtroom dynamics significantly. From financial records proving embezzlement to leaked emails that expose unethical negotiations, the gathered evidence can range dramatically in its nature and significance.

The defense, in a strategic move to counteract this barrage of incriminating evidence, may use their most potent weapon: public image. They may argue that the charges are politically motivated, or that the defendant has been trapped in a web of accusations due to their public standing. However, this weapon can very much backfire if the evidence is too overwhelming against them.

Another critical aspect of these trials is the role of the jury. Choosing and convincing this pool of unbiased citizens is crucial, and often considered an art in itself. The jury selection process, known as voir dire, includes extensive questioning about potential jurors' backgrounds, biases, and feelings about the defendant and the charges against him or her.

The defense and the prosecution both aim to form a jury that is receptive to their arguments. Notably, a jury in a high-profile case must also be able to withstand public scrutiny and media influence, maintaining their ability to deliver a fair and impartial verdict despite the surrounding buzz.

Then come the public's perception of the trial, which can cast a long shadow over the proceedings. In essence, there are two trials happening concurrently: the one in the courtroom, bounded by rules of law, and the one in the sphere of public opinion, driven by speculation, rumor, and emotion.

Despite the attention garnered by these trials, they are also subject to procedural fairness principles, ensuring that the defendant is receiving a fair and just trial. However, when the trial is held amidst a volatile public environment, striking a balance between open justice and fairness to the defendant becomes a significant challenge.

It's also worth noting that defense attorneys have to walk a fine line between defending their client and the potential reputational risk they take on. A high-profile case can make or break an attorney's career, and their decisions throughout the trial can have long-term consequences.

For the public servant turned defendant, their personal reputation isn't the only thing at stake. The impact of a guilty verdict could ripple out and affect their party, possibly even altering the political landscape. Therefore, these trials can serve as a litmus test for the body politic they come from or represent.

Lastly, while the trial may decide the public servant's legal fate, it's the court of public opinion that often decides their social fate. The trial may come to an end, but the memory of the public servant's fall from grace continues to echo in the annals of political history.

In conclusion, the trial of a public servant is more than just a legal proceeding. It's a spectacle that lays bare the duality of power and weakness, prompting us to reflect on the imperfections of those we entrust with our collective destiny. It's a stark reminder of the enduring principle that no one, no matter how influential, is above the law. It's a litmus test for our society's capacity for accountability, even towards those who once held its highest offices.

This trial is not just about an individual's fall from grace; it's about society's rise towards justice. The courtroom, echoing with arguments and counter-arguments, serves as an arena where democracy's strength is assessed, and where public servants' commitment to their oath is severely tested. In this arena, the chasm that separates a public servant and a defendant stands revealed, reminding us of the monumental responsibility and trust that comes with public office.

Sentencing: The Consequences of Conviction

Let's delve in. We've walked through the funhouse of power, studied the myriad crimes committed in the pursuit of it, and neurotically navigated the turbulent seas of the judicial process. Now we arrive, wearily but resolutely, at the concrete heart of consequences: the sentencing. Few things in life are as irrevocable and final as a sentence meted out by the forceful hand of justice. This moment, a junction in the life path of those who dared to misuse power, is densely packed with implications.

Should we perceive a criminal conviction as a tardy but well-deserved comeuppance or as a regretful loss of public trust? A situation already steeped in complex layers of morality, ethics, and law gets even murkier when confronted with this public ambiguity. To fully grasp the gravity of sentencing, it's crucial to unpack its core - the punishment and the message it sends, and secondly, its reverberating effects that ripple out into society.

First, though, let's address the vastly diverse sentencing options courts have at their disposal. Yes, indeed, judges aren't confined merely to banging gavels and decreeing prison terms. They have a potent arsenal of penalties to ensure that the punishment fits not only the crime but also matches its socio-economic context and impact on society. Probation, fines, restitution, community service, and imprisonment represent just the tip of the judicial iceberg.

A misconception worth dismantling here: prison isn't always the go-to option. Despite its notoriety in pop culture, imprisonment is often a last resort, used when the severity of the crime warrants such drastic measures. Lesser offenses may result in financial penalties, restitution to the victims, or service to the community. These, too, serve to rectify the wrongs, but without thrusting the offender into the grim recesses of a jail cell.

Alternatively, probation serves as a kind of testing period, an opportunity for offenders to demonstrate their capacity for rehabilitation in a monitored but relatively free environment. Yes, it's a shot at redemption, but the catch? One reckless mistake, one minor flouting of the law, and they're thrust back into the maelstrom of the judicial system.

Now, onto the potent symbol a sentence represents. The punishment meted out by the courts weighs heavily as a message of deterrence. It's a stern warning signal to others, effectively communicating that fraudulent pursuits of power, misuse of authority, or moral indiscretions won't go unchecked. It reinforces faith in the judiciary, underscoring its capabilities, and intent to ensure law enforcement and maintain societal equilibrium.

Then, there's the victim to consider. The consequences of sentencing stretch beyond the convicted, reaching the victims, either directly or indirectly affected. A harsh sentence often offers them justice, a sense of closure, and indeed a restoration of belief that the world is still ordered, not chaotic. Especially for those involved in high crimes and cases of an egregious breach of trust, a significant sentence can be the necessary counterweight to restore balance.

Sentencing impacts not just one individual or a group but the entire socio-political fabric of the country. It serves as a touchstone for societal values and norms, delineating what is acceptable behavior and what, decidedly, is not. It informs public conversation and shapes national sentiment.

However, the dark underbelly of this process is its potential for misuse. Sentencing can be weaponized to serve political agendas, to make scapegoats, or suppress dissenters, if left unchecked. It's yet another reason why an impartial, transparent judiciary is vital for a thriving democracy.

Moreover, sentencing leads to a cascade of effects, many unintended and unforeseen. Familial structures might shatter, communities could become frayed, and public faith can be eroded. The consequences reach long past the initial sentencing, extending into the lives irreparably changed by the conviction of a family member, a community leader, or a public servant.

Cognizant of these harsh realities, many courts are striving for a more holistic, equitable approach. The goal is not just punishment, but possibilities for restoration, rehabilitation, and reentry into society. Favoring reform over retribution is a prominent debate in legal circles, but as it stands, it's a discussion well worth having.

The echo of the gavel falling, signifying the concluding act in a drawn-out courtroom drama, can sometimes feel like a hasty end to a complex narrative. However, convict and sentence are much more than final acts; they are the early precursors of a cataclysm of consequences that follow. As we turn the page of this chapter and journey into the aftermath of a conviction, try to appreciate the magnitudes of these waves of changes set in motion by a single utterance: "Guilty as charged."

Hold onto your empathy, friends, as we are about to venture into the poignant realities suffered by those in the aftermath of conviction - the political, personal, and social fallout occurs post-sentencing, when the dust finally settles and the long path to redemption begins.

Chapter 5:
The Aftermath

As we delve into the aftermath of political crime, we can't help but grapple with its wide-ranging ripple effects. After the gavel falls, there's a dramatic ripple effect that flows outward from the sentences, impacting not only the convicted, but also the constituents – those everyday people who had once placed their faith in the hands of that now-fallen public servant. As the crime scene tape across the corridors of power comes down, we turn our attention to the fallout, which encompasses more than just the political landscape. It reverberates throughout society, seeping into our day-to-day conversations and shaking families to their core. The vacant seat left behind by the guilty begs the question: What comes next? This answer comes in various forms, most notably special elections and appointments, both of which have their own particular set of challenges and controversies. We watch as often unprepared successors step into the shoes once filled by charismatic, seasoned – albeit corrupt – leaders, struggling not to falter under the weight of the public's watchful eye. However, beyond the vacant seat and the political tumult, there exists the stark reality that our focus often steers clear of –the convict's life that continues, albeit tailored by the threads of stigma and disgrace. Where these individuals go from here, the paths they choose or the ones forced upon them, is a discourse often neglected, yet each holds powerful stories that offer deeper insights into the reality of power, corruption, and the aftermath of it all.

The Fallout: Political, Social, and Personal

There's an echo of shockwaves when a public servant falls from grace in the eyes of the law. It's a seismic event that impacts not only the individual, but society at large, and it can have lasting implications on the fabric of our democracy. Let's delve into these ramifications - political, social, and personal.

Politically, the fallout is immediate and substantial. The reputation of the public office the individual held is invariably tarnished, leading to public trust in that institution taking a nosedive. This lack of faith in government institutions is detrimental to a functioning democracy; it leads to disillusionment and apathy among voters, and that's without mentioning the power vacuum left in their wake.

This power vacuum renders the party of the disgraced public officer susceptible to fracture, creating a breeding ground for power struggles and internal conflicts. It's not uncommon for political opponents to use this as ammunition, to underscore corruption and decay within the party, further amplifying the fragility within the political landscape.

Moreover, policies or legislation initiated or endorsed by the convicted can face severe backlash, stymieing progress even if they might have been beneficial to the public. Voter confidence can falter, giving rise to skepticism of future legislation, even if untainted by scandal.

The social fallout, often underexamined, can be equally extensive. Scandals can spark necessary, but sometimes divisive, dialogues. As salacious details of criminal conduct make headlines, these spectacles feed into a cycle of sensationalism, which can blur the line between scrutinizing power and a public lynching.

Moreover, these scandals can also reinforce harmful stereotypes. For example, when influential individuals engage in unethical practices, it can perpetuate the perception that individuals in power are inherently corrupt. This may lead to far-reaching and unfounded suspicions about anyone who holds or seeks public office, further enervating public trust.

On the lighter side, such happenings can trigger a renewed interest in political engagement, prompting debates around integrity, corruption, and the nature of power. In this way, political scandals can indirectly promote active citizenship and an informed electorate.

The personal fallout for the convicted party is indeed heavy. Public disgrace, loss of personal reputation, and severed relationships are just a few of the consequences. A criminal convict can lose their livelihood and find opportunities closed off due to their conviction, potentially leading to economic hardships.

As a tragic irony, the pursuit and misuse of power that once elevated them, now isolates them. Public ridicule, along with the scorn exuded by political circles, can foster a profound sense of isolation. Many grapple with shame, regret, and a loss of identity after their fall from the peak of societal influence.

However, this reckoning can sometimes serve as a catalyst for profound personal and psychological change. Think of it as a crucible of transformation that gives rise to a stronger awareness of integrity, ethics, and the sense of responsibility vital to holding public office.

It's necessary to remember that these aftershocks don't only affect one individual but ripple throughout our society. As individuals, we must respond not with derision, but with a commitment to uphold the values that foster transparent government and responsible citizenship.

Looking at the political, social, and personal repercussions, we see the bigger picture gradually emerge. It's akin to assembling a complex jigsaw puzzle where every piece plays its part in creating a clearer understanding of the consequences of crimes committed in the public sphere.

This fallout underscores the profound impact that corrupt behaviors have on us all, not only serving as a cautionary tale for those entrapped in webs of deceit and wrongdoing but also for us, the public, reminding us of the crucial role we play in stewarding our democratic institutions.

The aftershocks of political scandals reverberate throughout society, morphing how we view power and the people we entrust it to. While it indeed paints a grim picture, let's not lose sight of the opportunity it presents - to engage, question, and ensure we rise to the challenge of creating a society that values integrity over individual gain.

The Vacant Seat: Special Elections and Appointments

It's inspiring, but perhaps a bit overwhelming, to learn about the power dynamics, missteps, and resulting judicial repercussions in the realm of American politics. When a public official falls from grace, leaving a vacant seat, a unique set of opportunities and challenges arises. This dynamic situation leads to both special elections and appointments, which is our area of focus for this section.

A public office is hardly ever simply abandoned in a vacuum; the vacant chair in the grandiose arena of American politics doesn't remain empty for long. It's as if the seat itself has a magnetic pull, attracting potential suitors eager to fill it and make their mark. Yet, the process to fill the void isn't as spontaneous as it may seem, but instead adheres to a well-established set of rules and traditions determined by layered and occasionally intertwined mechanisms known as special elections and appointments.

Let's start with special elections. Think of them as pop-up ballots, essentially unplanned votes triggered by an unexpected vacancy. They offer a real-time look into the current political climate of a region, like a barometer gauging atmospheric pressure. They usually occur after an official's sudden departure, such as a resignation, death, or removal from office for criminal actions.

Simultaneously concise yet intricate, special elections involve multi-stage procedures including primary elections to determine party nominees, followed by general elections between these candidates. In this way, special elections are a rapid-fire, condensed version of regular elections, staging a fierce competition and providing a platform for emerging political voices and agendas. Their short duration doesn't damper their significance; each carries weight as it influences the balance of power in government.

Yet, in some cases, special elections might not represent the electorate's will as comprehensively as regular ones. Participation tends to be low due to short notice and a lack of awareness among voters, making results potentially unrepresentative of broader sentiment. That isn't a critique of the mechanism, but an acknowledgment of its inherent limitations.

Some officials are fast-tracked into seats of power through another route: appointments. Depending on the context and jurisdiction, the responsibility to fill vacant seats may fall to a governor, a president, or legislative bodies. The appointment process sidesteps the electoral process, instead emphasizing the discernment and decision-making of a select few. This can expedite the process of filling vacancies, ensuring that government functions are not unduly hampered by empty seats.

Appointments have a veneer of simplicity compared to special elections, yet they're rife with controversy and implications. Are existing power structures merely reinforcing themselves? Does this bypass of a democratic vote compromise political accountability? These are only a few questions raised by this process.

To scrutinize appointments is to face a critique of elitism in democratic machinery. Appointments often disproportionately favor established politicians, elite academics, or corporate heavyweights, reinforcing the status quo and stifling diversity in political representation. Nonetheless, the process also allows for fast decision-making in times of crisis, a crucial function in a volatile world. Balancing these two aspects is a delicate act.

In many ways, assessing special elections and appointments is about engaging in the democratic process from all angles. It's coming to terms with the utter unpredictability of politics, the rapid shifts in power dynamics, and acknowledging the resilience of our democratic structures. It's understanding that these mechanisms, while challenging and sometimes controversial, are essential components of our political landscape.

By their nature, special elections and appointments illustrate the ongoing tension between efficiency and representation in democratic governance. On one hand, the need to promptly fill a void for the continuity of government services, on the other, the pressing demand to reflect the people's will accurately.

So, as the seat passes from one occupant to another, we observe not just the individual modifications to the schema of power but the reaffirmation of these critical democratic principles. Each shift in political occupancy is another chapter in the country's ongoing narrative of growth, learning, resolution, and reform. It's a testament to our democracy's ability to adapt, respond, and thrive amid adversity.

Just as the seat doesn't stay vacant for long, the influence and impact of these mechanisms do not cease once the seat is filled. Each appointment or special election reverberates outward, influencing the trajectory of individuals, parties, and politics. They are chapters within larger narratives, markers in the continually unfolding story of our democracy.

Whether it be the rapid response of a special election or the strategic maneuverings of an appointment, these areas of political process underscore a consistent truth: Democracy is not a static system but an ongoing work in progress. Our understanding and engagement with these processes speak to our shared commitment to a functioning, representative, and responsive democracy.

Life After Conviction: Where Do They Go From Here?

For convicted public servants, life after conviction presents a new reality, a stark shift from their previous positions of power and privilege. This isn't a simple shift in career or retiring from public life. It's a major, often challenging change in how they navigate society.

The path a convicted public official takes varies widely. Some manage to salvage their reputation to an extent and might even return to public life, while others fade into obscurity. Still, they all share one thing: a marked departure from their former influence.

Often, the first stop for individuals convicted of federal crimes is federal prison. Following sentencing, the Bureau of Prisons determines where an inmate will serve his or her term. Societal status and political clout, once considerably influential, carry little weight here. It's a stark, potent symbol of how dramatically their fortunes have shifted.

In prison, their former positions may impact their interactions with other inmates and staff. Other inmates may view them with a sense of curiosity or hostility, even as they adjust to the harsh realities of prison life themselves.

On the other hand, serving prison time is not the entirety of the post-conviction experience. Many public officials must also face a term of supervised release after they've served their sentences. Supervised release, during which individuals must regularly check in with a parole officer and abide by certain restrictions, is meant to aid in the transition back to society.

Some officials have attempted to resume their careers after serving their sentences, seeking a return to the public spotlight. Not surprisingly, this is met with varying degrees of success. Some manage to reenter politics or related fields, while others find that their past convictions make such a return near impossible.

When the path back to politics becomes impassable, some convicted officials turn to writing or public speaking, using these platforms to share their experiences or attempt to repair their public image. In some cases, they may use this platform to apologize for their actions or even to advocate for other individuals who have been involved in the criminal justice system.

Others retreat from public life entirely, seeking solace in their private lives with friends and family. They may resort to quieter occupations, transforming their experiences into cautionary tales.

Socially, these individuals often face a mixed reaction from their communities and society at large. On one hand, there can be sympathy or forgiveness from those who believe in their capacity for change and rehabilitation. Yet, they may also endure scorn, alienation, or indifference from others who view them as the personification of political corruption.

Unfortunately, for some ex-officials, the harsh realities of life after conviction prove too much to bear. Their mental health may deteriorate under the burden of public shame, reduced circumstances, and personal regret. In fact, the association between incarceration and poor mental health outcomes is well documented by researchers.

Critics argue that these challenges reflect the struggles faced by many released prisoners in America. They're slipping through society's cracks, their pasts hanging over them like a phantom, echoing the wider issue of prisoner reentry in the United States. Effective reintegration into society is a problem not unique to public officials and sparks a crucial conversation about reform and rehabilitation.

Some advocates argue that the post-conviction experience of public officials could serve as a powerful call to action, spotlighting the broader systemic issues with prison reintegration. Their high-profile cases could be used to advocate for reforms aimed at easing the transition from prison for all former inmates.

Whether their life after conviction leads to seclusion or redemption, to advocacy or despair, the journey underscores potent truths about fallibility, punishment, and resilience. It serves as a reminder that, ultimately, these individuals, once revered and admired, are as human and fallible as the rest of us.

Chapter 6:
Prevention and Solutions

In tackling the epidemic of questionable behavior in politics, a three-pronged approach may be effective: targeted institutional measures, assertive media scrutiny, and an actively engaged electorate. First, **Ethics Committees** serve as crucial internal regulators, operating as the very checks and balances vital in preserving integrity within administrative structures. Their scope extends to developing, enforcing, and reviewing ethical standards and codes of conduct, effectively wielding significant influence in curbing unethical behaviors early on. Meanwhile, **media**, often termed the 'Fourth Estate', embraces a pivotal role of holding power to account. Polished investigative journalism can expose corruption, present it to the public eye, and exacerbate the consequences for those involved, hence preventing others from straying into similar misconducts. Lastly, the **voter's role** cannot be overstated. Public vigilance serves as the foundation for a successful democracy; voters' awareness, their willingness to demand transparency, and holding their leaders accountable can work wonders in arresting the tide of corruption. This shared responsibility, between institutional safeguards, the media, and the voting public, can potentially pave the way for a cleaner, more accountable political arena.

Ethics Committees: Internal Checks and Balances

Critical components within any respectable organization, not least within the arena of politics, are the Ethics Committees. They serve as internal checks and balances, ensuring that -

well, rather, endeavoring to ensure, that actions and decisions fall within parameters of propriety. No system is foolproof, but their role is to make it as immune as possible to breaches of ethical conduct.

Gravitas in character and integrity in service, these are the standards of behavior that elected officials are expected to uphold. To these attributes, the Ethics Committees are the compasses, the guiding principles that key decision-makers are required to follow.

Internal checks and balances, the meat and muscles of democracy, prevent any single individual or group from wielding undue influence, thereby promoting fairness and impartiality. The system of checks and balances deter corruption, mitigate the risk of abuse of power, and set a logical framework for ethical behavior.

So what happens when someone veers from the path of righteousness? Who ensures that errant actions meet with just consequences? This is where the Ethics Committee steps in, the watchman in the wings, ever vigilant.

Consisting of peers within the setting, whether it's a committee in Congress or in a nonprofit organization, the Ethics Committee peruses any conduct that may be of questionable ethics. They are the custodians of moral correctness, the guardians who oversee integrity in practice. Their mandate is to uphold the tenets of accountability and honesty, to protect the symbol of trust that public service represents.

But let's cut to the chase; the presence of an Ethics Committee doesn't preclude ethical mishaps, Committee or no Committee. That's a fact. We cannot control every act, particularly those shrouded in secrecy. However, the existence of a committee does make it significantly harder for those acts to remain hidden and adds a level of deterrence against misconduct. It's a preventative, as much as it is a curative, measure.

The Ethics Committee instigates investigations when irregularities appear. They review documents, call for witnesses, and interrogate persons of interest. They have the power to recommend disciplinary actions, ranging from a slap on the wrist to full-blown expulsions. They can, and do, serve as the jury and judge.

Committees vary in their execution of tasks, often reflecting the culture and attitudes of the place they serve. Some can be proactive, diligently monitoring for any signs of impropriety. Others might be reactive, coming into action only when serious missteps have been committed.

You might wonder if having peers as members of an Ethics Committee could lead to inconsistency, partiality, or hesitation in meting out penalties. That's a fair concern, as human nature can succumb to alliances, friendships, and personal vested interests.

However, the inherent strength of these committees is their reliance on collective decision-making. Decisions are less likely to be influenced by individual bias, more likely to be the result of sober, reasoned debate. Of course, it's imperative that members on these committees have a high level of integrity themselves, are not swayed by emotions or personal gain, and understand the enormity of their role in upholding ethical conduct.

For all their virtues, Ethics Committees are not magical solutions. They don't guarantee an absence of corruption, and they can't always uncover hidden misdeeds. But, they are an integral part of a larger puzzle. Without them, the system has less oversight and less accountability - two crucial elements to keep a democracy robust and progressive.

At the end of the day, Ethics Committees epitomize the old adage, 'eternal vigilance is the price of liberty'. They serve as a reminder, to themselves and to us, that their unwavering commitment to upholding the principles of truth, ethics, and integrity is the shield that protects democracy from its potential downfall.

Ultimately, internal checks and balances like Ethics Committees demonstrate a commitment to play by the rules, to operate with fairness and integrity, and to punish those who do not. They help preserve faith in our democratic institutions giving voters hope that the system can indeed self-correct.

Although not the most glamorous side of politics, these committees play an indispensable role in maintaining a healthy democracy. By continually striving for a more transparent and accountable political environment, they aid in pushing boundaries and setting ever higher standards for those in power.

The Role of the Media: Holding Power to Account

The Fourth Estate, known colloquially as the media, performs a critical role in the democratic process. In the age-old contest of power and governance, the media's function cannot be overstated. They shine a spotlight on the holders of power, scrutinizing their every move, every word, and every decision, looking through the lens of accountability. Without the exhaustive efforts of journalists, broadcasters, and editors, the public would be left to the mercy of smoke-and-mirror games played in the corridors of power.

The media is the figurative mirror held against society, reflecting the intricate workings of our political and social systems. This mirror's clarity and accuracy, though often skewed by various biases and influences, remains vital for maintaining democratic checks and balances. By holding public representatives to account, the media attempts to create a culture of honesty, transparency, and responsibility.

Unveiling corruption and misuse of power, the media has left an indelible mark on the political landscape. Their investigative work often exposes intricate webs of deceit that, otherwise, might have remained hidden. Journalistic exposés spotlight scandals, helping to bring about the punishments detailed in previous chapters. These pursuits of truth and justice occur in the backdrop of great personal and professional risk, standing testament to the vital role media plays.

However, holding power to account isn't simply about showcasing public wrongdoings. It also means representing the truth and nuanced perspectives of complex geopolitical situations. For example, the media's role in reporting on international crisis zones, armed conflicts, or political disarray is instrumental in shaping public opinion and affecting policy changes.

Given the media's influence, it's crucial that they remain independent. After all, a press beholden to the powerful quickly loses its capacity for criticism and objectivity. Promoting press freedom and safeguarding the integrity of journalistic institutions are, therefore, of paramount importance.

However, media independence doesn't mean complete isolation. Journalists rely on wide networking webs, drawing information from well-placed sources, whistleblowers, and insiders. Their complex relationships within political circles further fuel their watchdog role.

History is filled with cases where the media, armed with perseverance and dogged determination, has exposed widespread corruption. Reporters wielding notepads and cameras have brought down politicians insulated by power, their stories acting as battering rams against previously impervious walls of deceit.

One cannot but admire the sheer audacity of the media in challenging the mighty and the powerful. Still, their role in holding power to account isn't without controversies. Issues concerning media ethics, sensationalism, and alleged bias often muddy the waters, sparking debates about the media's responsibility and the limits of press freedom.

In today's digital age, the role of the mainstream media in maintaining accountability has faced new challenges. The advent of social media platforms, often riddled with misinformation and 'fake news', has led to a crisis of credibility. Meanwhile, the age-old problem of media consolidation or ownership by a few wealthy individuals or corporations continues to raise questions about the objectivity of many news organizations.

Regardless, the media's seminal role in democratic societies remains mostly unchallenged. It serves as the people's eyes and ears, navigating the labyrinthine world of politics on their behalf. Its articles, broadcasts, and documentaries illuminate the dark corners of government decisions, ensuring the powerful can never comfortably relax into unscrutinized activity.

To that effect, cultivating media literacy, encouraging transparency, and advocating for journalistic freedoms are the need of the hour. These measures ensure that the media stands strong against the wind and does not succumb to the pressures of power.

In the grand chessboard of power and governance, the media remains an essential player. Its role as a watchdog, bearing witness, and raising alarms cannot be downplayed. It empowers the people with knowledge, demystifying the complex mechanics of political power, and revealing both the virtue and vulnerability of those we elect to serve us.

However, in order to curate an informed and engaged public, the media must continually evolve to meet new challenges. It must learn, grow, and adapt to preserve its vital role in bringing accountability to power. Just as power seeks to silence and control, the media must always stride forward, raising its collective voice against corruption, misinformation, and abuses of power.

In essence, a robust and independent media industry is the lifeblood of a vibrant democracy. It is a pillar supporting the integrity of our political institutions, challenging the powerful, and leading the charge for accountability. It is, put simply, the guardian of democracy, tasked with the critical duty of ensuring that those who govern us do so in our best interest.

Public Vigilance: The Role of Voters

In a thriving democracy, the populace, that is, the voters act as a bulwark against the abuse of power. The voter's role is pivotal in maintaining transparency, fostering accountability, and ultimately, combating corruption in public office. Unfortunately, despite its significance, this role is often undervalued or misunderstood by many.

Voters have much more control than they often realize. They're not just passively accepting or rejecting a moot point at a polling station. They're actually participating in shaping the political landscape. An enlightened and erudite electorate that stays informed about the political discourse can advance the cause of justice and transparency.

Voting isn't limited to choosing an individual or a party every four years. It's a continuous process that involves staying updated about the political scenario, learning about the governance model, and understanding the policies and laws that impact society. A vote, in essence, is a citizen's opinion on governance directed towards a better future.

We can't emphasize enough that information is vital. The significance of having access to reliable, impartial information to help us form a reasoned opinion can't be overstated. An informed voter is more likely to make rational decisions and isn't easily swayed by fake news or propaganda, hence promoting healthier outcomes.

The Power of the Ballot

Voters hold the power to either validate or resist the actions of their representatives through the ballot. This power is one of the most consequential democratic tools for ordinary citizens, enabling them to hold public officials accountable.

If the people in power think that voters aren't vigilant, they might be tempted to misuse their office for personal gains. On the other hand, an engaged electorate can deter such misadventures. Simply by casting a vote, amazing transformations can occur on both local and national scales.

But for the power of the ballot to really make a difference, it needs to be used judiciously and responsibly. It's not enough to vote based on party affiliations or to follow ancestral political loyalties. Each and every vote needs to be a well thought out decision, based on the integrity and track record of the individual in question.

The Role of Participation

To ensure that the democratic process truly represents their needs and desires, it's vital for voters to participate actively in the process. Participation includes turning out to vote in every election, becoming involved in party politics or non-partisan civic engagement, volunteering during campaigns, and even running for office.

Public meetings and town halls provide opportunities to question elected representatives directly. Similarly, civic movements, protests, and digital activism also serve as platforms for voters to express their views and make their voices heard.

Critical Thinking

Active voters don't just participate, they think critically. It's a responsibility of the electorate to analyze promises made by politicians, scrutinize their track records, and consider their credibility before casting a vote. This necessitates an inherent skepticism towards those in power and a commitment to independent thinking.

Contrary to creating division, this critical thinking helps to ensure understanding and consensus around shared values and goals. This leads to a more collaborative political environment, a degree of political unity, and increased trust in the democratic process.

Accountability Beyond Election Day

Accountability doesn't end on election day. In fact, the role of the voter extends far beyond casting ballots. It's essential to stay abreast of the activities of the elected officials and to continue to hold them accountable for their actions throughout their tenure.

Communication with elected officials between elections can send a clear message that the voters are actively engaged and keeping tabs on their actions. Attending public meetings, sending letters or emails, and using social media are effective means to demand accountability and promote transparency.

Conclusion

After all, the ultimate objective of democracy is to create a just and fair society. And it's important to remember that our participation as voters doesn't guarantee a perfect government, but it certainly makes it much more likely.

In the end, public vigilance through active, informed voting is a key element in preventing corruption and ensuring the integrity of public office. As voters, we share a collective responsibility for both our present realities and the shape of our future. So, let's embrace our role and dutifully contribute to the upkeep of the democratic process.

Conclusion

In our journey through the landscape of American power
and political corruption, we've gained insights into the
allure, mechanisms, and potential solutions to these
pressing issues. We've delved into the psychology of those
seeking power, explored the broad range of crimes
committed by those in office, and studied the complex
judicial process that holds them accountable. But as we've
seen, these realities still persist. The question, then, is: how
can we use what we've learned to stem the tide of corruption,
and work towards a cleaner political horizon?

First, we've seen burdening evidence of how the allure of
power can potentially warp a person's convictions and
judgement when serving in public office. Power does not
breed corruption directly, but it can invite temptation and
blur ethical lines. This revelation underscores the
importance of electing leaders with a strong moral compass,
demonstrating that character traits such as integrity,
humility, and transparency are pivotal in those who hold our
nation's highest offices.

We analyzed the different types of crimes committed by
those in power, from the quietly insidious acts like bribery
and embezzlements, to the higher end of the crime spectrum
with treason and espionage. Understanding the wide range
of such offences, it becomes clear the framework for
corruption is not one-dimensional. This further reinforces
the need for strong structural safeguards and vigilance on
every level of governance.

We also learned that corruption follows certain mechanisms,
often hidden beneath the surface. Lobbyists, campaign

finance, and patronage have all shown to be volatile instruments that can be exploited under the right circumstances. While these elements are not inherently corrupt, their potential for misuse necessitates legislation to increase transparency and accountability in these areas.

The judicial process can seem like a tangled web, but it's where justice ultimately checks the balance. Investigating and indicting culprits, with trials often played out in the public eye, is a high-stakes process. Missteps can result in the guilty walking free, while a well-conducted investigation and trial can serve as a potent deterrent to public servants who might be tempted to stray.

The aftermath of political corruption shows just how wide-ranging and deep the fallout can be. It doesn't just affect the individual involved, but the office they held, their colleagues, and most importantly, the public trust in the institution.

However, by looking at the vacant seats left behind, we can see the resilience of our political system. Special elections and appointments provide opportunities for fresh faces who can learn from the past and strive to serve their constituents honestly. Moreover, seeing the convicted offenders navigate life after their conviction serves as a sobering reminder to those in power that no one is beyond reproach.

Evaluating preventative measures and insights into potential solutions has certainly been enlightening. Ethics committees, media watchdog groups, and public vigilance form the three prongs of a check-and-balance system aimed to curtail corruption.

Through understanding these scenarios and themes, we can adapt our decisions, enhance our skepticism, and ultimately contribute to a healthier democracy. With greater accountability from our elected officials and from ourselves as voters, we have a chance at reducing the frequency and intensity of these instances of corruption.

The role of education and awareness cannot be overstated; understanding the ins-and-outs of our political system allows us to identify when something isn't right. However, it's equally important to remember that while we discuss these instances of corruption, the majority of our public servants still work diligently and honestly for their constituents.

Looking to the future, we must ask ourselves: Can we stem the tide? The answer to this lies in our collective hands and minds. If we, as citizens, seek out information, question the status quo, and hold our representatives accountable, we surely can make progress.

There have been many casualties on the road to exposing corruption, from shattered reputations and careers to public trust in our institutions. However, remember that every exposed act of corruption brings us closer to a clean political landscape, as long as we learn from it, act on it, and ensure it doesn't happen again.

Our journey through this exploration of American political corruption brings us full circle to the place we started: with power. It can uplift or corrupt, unite or divide, create or destroy. If wielded properly, power can be a force for good. And while the path to that ideal may be fraught with challenges, it's a journey worth undertaking for the sake of our future.

So let's endeavor to continue to hold our elected officials accountable, stay active in local and national politics, and commit to making transparency and integrity standard expectations. After all, it's a democracy, where power truly belongs to the people. Let's ensure it serves us, and not the other way around.

85

Appendix:
A Brief History of Political Crime in America

As we shift our gaze back to the roots of our nation, we find instances of political crimes which have had a significant influence on how our politics functions today. During the 1700s, American politics was raw and untouched, marked by the birth pangs of the nation — yet political transgressions were not absent. Fraudulent voting and false counting in elections were early challenges during this period, setting a precedent that political crime was not an anachronism in our journey as a country. Moving into the 1800s, political crime grew in complexity, as the formative decades saw cases of corruption, embezzlement, and bribery become a steady part of the landscape. The Tweed Ring scandal of the 1860s, led by New York's Boss Tweed, was the epitome of corruption and greed during this time. The 1900s marked an era where high crimes such as treason and espionage became more prevalent, just as the Teapot Dome scandal and Watergate in the 1970s demonstrated. Hence, political figures somehow found ways to abuse their power even in the face of more explicit laws and stricter oversight. As we turned into the 2000s, and the age of technology further morphed the style and substance of political crime with cybercrimes, including email hacking scandals and questions over campaign funding began to dominate headlines. In summing up, political crimes have been a consistent strain in American history, evolving with the times, capricious in their nature, and presenting new challenges as society advances. Our understanding of these crimes and committed efforts to combat them will indeed shape our future political climate.

1700s

As the newborn American republic took its first hesitant steps on the global stage in the 1700s, the seeds of political crime were sown. It wasn't all tea parties and revolutionary fervor; behind the patriotic narrative, power struggles and improper acts quickly became part of the fabric of the political landscape.

Contrary to a widely held romantic kind of nostalgia, the Founding Fathers weren't immune to the influence of power or moral blunders. However, the pervasive nature of political corruption as we understand it today was still in its infancy. Often, actions weren't considered illicit or unethical simply because the measures to define and deter such acts weren't in place yet. A growing nation has a lot on its plate with matters such as statehood, constitution drafting, and war recovery.

Establishing an entirely new form of governance required immense dedication, humility, and, most importantly, integrity. Sadly, though, history doesn't often lend itself to such spotless narratives. Even during these embryonic stages in American history, the propensity for power to corrupt shone through.

The nascent federal and state governments quickly became embroiled in issues of boundary disputes and land speculation, often involving high-ranking officials. Wealth, status, and power became inseparable in an era where land meant all three. These blurred lines between public interests and personal gain paved the way for the types of political crimes we're all too familiar with today.

Customs positions, too, were often leveraged by individuals as a pathway to self-enrichment. Fees and taxes collected were all too often pocketed by unethical officials, an early instance of financial crimes in the budding American bureaucracy.

The 1700s also bore witness to the first murmurs of lobbying, albeit not in the systematic fashion that we know today. Wealthy individuals and corporations would appeal directly to lawmakers for legislation favoring their interests – a subtle form of power abuse that transformed into an organized whole over the centuries.

However, despite these early instances of political impropriety, many historical figures endeavored to uphold the values of the fledgling nation, epitomizing public service's honor. They aimed to establish a strong framework to keep the influence of power in check and to serve the people above all else.

Extensive debates and caution were employed when formulating the Constitution, which acted as the country's first solid defense against corruption and abusive behaviors. The division of powers, checks and balances, and a judicial review system were installed to deter individuals from using their offices for personal gain.

Such measures were a testament to the Founding Fathers' insight that power could tempt even the most virtuous individuals. Their efforts didn't fully eradicate political crime, but they laid the groundwork for the rule of law in the United States.

However, while steps were made to build defenses against corruption, the focus remained heavily on the workings of the federal government, leaving state implementations to the courts, a system that harbored its own set of complexities and pitfalls.

While the 1700s weren't without their share of political missteps and moral failings, it was also a time when critical legislative and cultural foundations were laid down. Institutions were erected to balance power, ethical standards were set into motion, and dawning awareness about the nature of corruption was fostered among the public.

Despite the era's shortcomings, it was a significant period in shaping the American approach to political integrity and the rule of law. It formed the bedrock over which the arenas of political crime, unethical behavior, and their persecution would evolve in the centuries to come.

In a sense, the 1700s set the stage for the ongoing struggle between power and accountability - a theme that would resonate through the tumultuous chapters of American history that were yet to be written.

Over time, the political landscape of America, much like its people and culture, evolved and matured. But, as we'll see in the discussion of the following centuries, some things - including the persistence of political crime and power abuse - remained constant.

1800s

The 1800s in American history were, to put it mildly, a unique confluence of evolving politics, groundbreaking social change, and seismic shifts in ideological landscapes. Oh, and we can't forget the incidents of political crime that are at the heart of our discourse. The lure of power, like the mythical Siren's song, was just as potent then as it is today.

Expansion was the name of the game, and the vast territorial growth gave rise to various complexities, including those around power capacities. In a landscape where political boundaries were literally being redrawn, the palpable sense of corruption was hard to ignore.

On the east coast, the emerging world of industrial capitalism presented a fertile ground for financial crimes. In Washington, D.C., the halls of power buzzed with the potential for abuse. Political machine run cities like New York saw spectacular scandals at every turn. James "Slippery Jim" Fisk and William "Boss" Tweed left behind legacies that are still studied by criminologists today. Innovation, it seems, wasn't strictly limited to the technological realm.

And let's not forget, the 1800s was an era of monumental social change, the greatest perhaps being the abolition of slavery. The Civil War not only divided the nation geographically, but also along morally ambiguous lines. For some, the seismic ideological shifts were manipulated for political gain. This decade was far from bereft of moral failings in political circles returning to the limelight.

To clarify, this isn't to minimize the cataclysmic cost that came with this change - the American Civil War was as much about corruption as it was about slavery. We speak of "high crimes" in the modern sense, but let's spare a moment for the egregious deeds of this pivotal time: political and financial manipulations, the press-ganging of troops, and the exploitation of a freed yet disenfranchised populace.

Against this backdrop emerged mechanisms of corruption that still resonate. The spoils system thrived, an unseemly kind of patrimonial politics where loyalty was frequently bought and sold. And not to be outdone, disruptive innovations in communication technology (hello, telegraph!)

gave new tools to those seeking to manipulate public sentiment.

Meanwhile, the judiciary was wrestling with its own identity. The court systems were still relatively youthful and shaping their processes while dealing with such ominous cases. The bridge from public servant to defendant was often gilded with unscrupulous acts, leading to trials that carry a certain historic weight to this day.

The aftermath of these acts of political crime left discernible traces on the fabric of American society, a dramatic fallout that reshaped the political dynamics of the era. Look around, and we still see the vacant seats, the special elections, and the indelible mark left on political families and parties.

Yet, it is essential to remember the individuals who tasted the bitter gall of criminal conviction and came to understand the reality of life after power. The disgrace of political failure, the deafening silence when the cheering crowds disperse, and the judicial consequences served as stern reminders of the limits of public service.

There were, however, glimmers of hope in this tumultuous century. Ethics committees began to find their voice, providing that essential internal check on the behavior of elected officials. Similarly, the burgeoning media industry, armed with the mighty pen and the telegraph, reminded those in power that their actions were not above scrutiny.

And what about the ordinary citizens? As always, they played a crucial role in shaping the political discourse of the 1800s. While the public vigilance may have lacked today's tools - no social media hashtags then! - it was a force one simply couldn't ignore. Their criticisms, protests, and votes served as the clarion call for accountability, reminding us of the power and responsibility of the ordinary citizen in a democracy.

In conclusion, the 1800s were a crucible of contradictory forces. We saw insatiable ambition colliding with an increased call for accountability. Yet within this turmoil, we find lessons: the cost of unchecked power, the price of moral compromise, and the value of public vigilance. It's a reflection that mires us in the muddy reality of our past, but also grants us understanding that better inform our present and future stages of political integrity.

1900s

During the 20th century, the United States grew into the global superpower that it is today. However, as the country expanded, so did the scope of political crimes. The dawn of the century brought improvements in technology, the rise of the mass media, and sweeping societal changes — each providing new opportunities for corruption.

For instance, advancement in communication methods through the advent of television affected the political landscape immensely. The overall reach and impact of politicians extended beyond their local constituencies to impact nationwide audiences. However, this increased visibility also ushered in new opportunities for those with less than honorable intentions.

From a broader spectrum, systemic corruption was rampant at the local and state levels throughout the early 20th century. Civic governments were frequently bogged down by the influence of political machines, which exchanged public resources and favors for loyalty and votes. Political bosses, like the infamous William M. Tweed or "Boss Tweed" of

Tammany Hall, dominated the scene, manipulating public sentiment for their personal gains.

The Prohibition era of the 1920s also brought about a particular surge in political corruption. Ill-equipped to handle the sudden illegality of alcohol, many law enforcement officers, public officials, and politicians were either complicit in or directly involved in the glitzy, albeit criminal, underworld of speakeasies and bootlegging.

The mid-century saw the very foundations of our democracy tested in dramatic fashion. The 1950s brought the rise of McCarthyism, a destructive campaign led by Senator Joseph McCarthy to root out suspected communists within the government and society. These tactics, reading something like a chilling, noir crime thriller, consisted of exaggerated accusations, public humiliations, topped off by a sprinkle of baseless, but toxic allegations, thus staining many innocent lives with unfounded charges of treason.

These threads of corruption and abuse of power, already woven into the fabric of American politics, further materialized in the 1970s with the Watergate scandal. Orchestrated by operatives within the highest ranks of the government, the burglary at the Democratic National Committee headquarters eventually led to the first-ever resignation of a sitting U.S. president. This marked a severe test of our democratic system's resilience, and sparked a fervent desire for reform.

The 1980s and '90s, however, were not exempt from political misconduct. These decades saw an increasing use of sophisticated financial schemes by public servants for personal enrichment, highlighting the growing connection between money and political power. From the 'Abscam' scandal, that led to the conviction of several members of

Congress, to less known but equally egregious instances of criminal misconduct involving bribery, campaign finance fraud, and extortion, the close of the 20th century emphasized the necessity for a systemic revamp in political ethics.

There were also instances of moral failings that blurred the lines between personal indiscretions and political corruption. Instances where politicians leveraged their positions to suppress scandals, intimidate victims, or manipulate the media spotlight, underscored the potential misuse of power, by those we place in positions of trust.

Yet, despite this grim panorama, the 20th century also brought significant strides towards improving the nation's handle on political corruption. Advances in technology and the growth of investigative media contributed to enhanced public awareness. Political scandals were more likely to be exposed, and corrupt officials faced increasing scrutiny.

Moreover, several legislative and institutional mechanisms were introduced during this period to counteract corruption. These included the Ethics in Government Act following Watergate, the establishment of independent ethics committees, and more rigorous campaign finance laws. The role of the Federal Election Commission grew more critical in averting any possible political malfeasance. Simultaneously, these developments catalyzed a higher expectation among citizens for their elected officials' ethical conduct.

Nevertheless, as the century drew to a close, it became apparent that while we had managed to put some checks on corruption, the battle was far from over. The increasing complexity of political crimes, coupled with the ever-changing societal and technological landscapes, reflected the need for proactive vigilance and adaptation. Transparency, accountability, and ethical conduct were no longer mere ideals, but prerequisites to maintaining a healthy democracy.

To summarize, the 20th century offers a complex tableau of political corruption and reform. Its lessons – those of endurance, resilience, and the unyielding pursuit of justice – serve as a stark reminder of our responsibility as citizens. The takeaways are clear: we must strive to understand history to better grapple with the present, to navigate the complexities of power and prevent such misconduct from recurring in future decades.

The subsequent chapters will delve deeper into the individual mechanisms of corruption, the judicial process, and potential preventative measures that can be put into place. However, the foundation laid down by studying the 1900s offers a thorough understanding of the evolution of American political crime, and leads us onto a roadmap for future reform.

2000s

As the grimy layers of past eras were peeled back in America's political landscape, the 21st century dawned with fresh promises of transparency and accountability. But beneath this glossy veneer, the 2000s brought their share of notorious political crimes to light.

Financial misdeeds simmered below the surface of public awareness, their roots buried in a labyrinth of political connections, extravagant campaign finances, and a culture of economic boom. Despite the supposed advancements both in the legal framework and societal vigilance, high-profile corruption cases reminded us that graft is not just a relic of an unenlightened past, but a stubborn stain on the fabric of politics that needs continuous attention.

It can't be overstated how much of an impact the Internet and digital communications had on the political scene in the 2000s. Where physical backroom deals were once the norm, now covert online communications and encoded email exchanges became the modern conduits of corruption. These electronic breadcrumbs often became the evidence used in investigations that uncovered instances of bribery, abuse of power, and other forms of political malfeasance.

The 2000s also introduced the global arena into play. It wasn't just domestic crimes that were under the scanner anymore; we had cases reaching out across international borders, ensnaring foreign nationals in their web. Cases of espionage were no longer confined to frosty Cold War narratives; they evolved into cybercrimes, data breaches, and complex instances of geopolitical skullduggery.

Scandals of personal indiscretions hit the headlines with uncomfortable regularity, testing the limits of public tolerance. The ethical conundrum these created raised a pertinent question: where should one draw the line between a public figure's professional responsibilities and their private actions? As one wonders, the skeletons kept tumbling out of closets, undeterred by the chorus of public outcry.

Campaign finance continued to play a pivotal yet murky role in determining political power dynamics. Instances of corruption were uncovered, where undisclosed amounts were funneled to bolster candidates or to disfavor opponents. Quashing the notion that money is peripheral to the pursuit of power, these instances painfully reaffirmed its deep-rooted influence, further muddying the waters of American politics.

The very systems that were designed to protect ethical practice in government were often implicated in these matters too. Internal checks and balances were revealed to be less than watertight, with ethics committees coming under scrutiny for conflicts of interest. In some instances, power's corrosive force seemed to have compromised the independence of these investigative arms, obscuring the demarcation between watchdog and accomplice.

Yet, amidst the cascading avalanche of misconduct, there were positive undercurrents emerging in this era. Public vigilance began to gain unprecedented value as citizens, armed with the power of technology, participated actively in scrutinizing their leaders.

The role of media extended beyond mere reporting to deeper investigative exposition of concealed political narratives. Cases of corruption made primetime news, and the metamorphosis of print, electronic, and digital media profoundly transformed the way such narratives were perceived, digested, and acted upon by the public.

And then, we had the trials. Public servants morphed into defendants in courtroom dramas that played out on national television. While some saw this as a disheartening theater of fallen heroes, others saw it as a beacon of hope, affirming the fact that no one is above the law, not even the most influential figures in politics.

Post-conviction, it was fascinating to watch the ripples spread out. Political, social, and personal fallout from these crimes impacted not just the individuals implicated, but the collective psyche of the nation. Special elections and appointments had to be held, and the trajectory of many a professional life was dramatically altered in their aftermath.

The 2000s affirmed that the fight against corruption is a continuous pursuit. As technology advances rapidly, the manifestations of corruption evolve contemporaneously. What we uncover sometimes may just be the tip of the iceberg, but it serves as a stark reminder that vigilance, transparency and accountability are the bulwarks against the encroachment of political corruption.

As we examine this era, we should be less interested in pointing fingers at fallen individuals and more focused on understanding the broader systems that allowed for such conduct to occur. Only then can we genuinely hope to unravel the Gordian knot of corruption, making durable changes that clearly delineate power's road from ambition to accountability, rather than concealment and malfeasance.

In the final analysis, the 2000s showed that American society is capable of facing these vexatious issues head-on. As disheartening as it might be to continually unearth instances of political malfeasance, it's also illuminating that the nation's systems of accountability often bear fruit. As we proceed into the future, it's our collective responsibility to nurture these systems and ensure they remain effective in curbing political crime.

Thomas T. Taylor